ROD
RAGE

ROD RAGE

To Bob —
One of my fly
fishing heroes!!
Rhea Topping
Denver 2004

EDITED BY

Rhea Topping

THE LYONS PRESS
Guilford, Connecticut
An imprint of the The Globe Pequot Press

The Lyons Press is an imprint of The Globe Pequot Press.

10 9 8 7 6 5 4 3 2 1

Printed in the United States of America

Designed by Peter Holm, Sterling Hill Productions

ISBN 1-59228-552-X

Library of Congress Cataloging-in-Publication data is available on file.

This book is dedicated to the people who have most influenced my adult life and my fly fishing:

CAROLE MILLER
my best friend and fishing partner,
who ignited the fires.

JOAN WULFF
my mentor and dear friend, who believed in me,
and who instilled in me a passion for fly casting and teaching.

— and to —

MR. MAGOO
who knows how very important he is to me.

"Angling was once a sport of a few quiet men. At various times it has been considered immoral, self-indulgent, degenerate; at others, a harmless aberration, justifying mildly humorous persecution. There must have been times, too, when no one paid very much attention and the quiet men were left to go their quiet ways in peace; these were probably the best times of all."

RODERICK HAIG-BROWN

"Bad tempers are on display everywhere. The examples we are setting for our kids is terrible. The media reports incidences of road rage, airplane rage, biker rage, surfer rage, grocery store rage, and even rage at youth sports activities. There is a general breakdown of social conventions, of manners. This gives a validation, a permission, to be aggressive. Our lives are crumpled up with stress, multi-tasking, high expectations, lack of manners. Social scientists say we are in the midst of a new epidemic of anger that, in its mildest forms, is unsettling, and, at its worst, turns deadly."

USA Today, July 18, 2000

"A recent *U.S. News & World Report* study showed that 89 percent of Americans feel civility has hit a new low and that we are ready for a change."

USA Today, May 26–29, 2000

CONTENTS

II. Modern Sensibility

III. Oceans, Flats, and Salt Water

IV. Of Boats and Guides

V. Salmon and Steelhead

VII. A Way of Life

ACKNOWLEDGMENTS

Without help and encouragement from the following people, this book would never have been completed. This is "our" book.

ALL THE CONTRIBUTORS
DAVE BRANDT
MARY BROOKS
JAY CASSELL
HELEN CLARK
SHELL GAUMOND
VALERIE HAIG-BROWN
THE KEMPHS
LEFTY KREH
GLENN LAW
JEFF PILL
JUDITH SCHNELL
CAM SIGLER
GENE TRUMP
THE CATSKILL FLY FISHING CENTER
THE AMERICAN MUSEUM OF FLY FISHING
THE ATLANTIC SALMON FOUNDATION
THE FEDERATION OF FLY FISHERS

And to all my family and friends who put me up, and put up with me, during the past seven years of working on this book. Thank you very, very much!

INTRODUCTION

*Th*is book is dedicated to the lady with the white Range Rover, whom I blasted for wading in front of me many years ago on the Jackson River . . . my sincere apologies.

And to all future fly fishers: I hope this book will help to maximize the pleasure which might be derived from the unique and rewarding sport of angling through knowledge, courtesy, patience, responsibility, and common sense.

With the ever-increasing popularity of fly fishing, we are finding overcrowding in all of our rivers, streams, creeks, oceans, estuaries, lakes, and ponds. Without explicit rules or guidelines, we more and more often find ourselves infringing on each other's time, space, and enjoyment. Only through education and awareness can we become cognizant of nurturing respect for each other, for the fish, and for the environment.

As my own angling has progressed, I continue to find myself in uncompromising situations, where I am unsure not so much, nowadays, of the correct protocol but rather how to avoid or resolve confrontational situations.

During the research stage of this book, I began seeking the counsel of veteran fly fishermen, and I found that although there are no rules set in stone, they each had an opinion of how best to handle various difficult situations, and they were delighted to contribute to a book which was finally going to address these issues. This book is a compilation of their colorful anecdotes, observations, and suggestions.

As I had the good fortune to travel and fish in other countries, I became aware that customs differed greatly in each place. This led me to include a section on fly fishing protocol for some of the more popularly fished areas in foreign countries as well.

One of the most significant lessons I have gleaned on my personal road to becoming a better angler came from my mentor, Joan Wulff, who said, "We should all try to give something back to this wonderful sport." This book on fly fishing etiquette is my attempt to do just that.

My sincere hope for the future of fly fishing is that fly shops, guides, the Park Service and other governmental agencies, boat rental companies, and every one of us who loves the sport will enjoy these stories and pass on an awareness of the importance of fly fishing etiquette.

WHY DO PEOPLE FISH?
Casting to the Bottom of Angling Etiquette

MEL KRIEGER
San Francisco, California

Mel Krieger has taught literally thousands of people to fly fish in the past forty years. He has conducted the Mel Krieger International Fly Fishing School throughout the world. His book, *The Essence of Flycasting*, and his videos, *The Essence of Flycasting I* and *II, Beginnings*, and *The Essence of Spey Casting*, have been translated into many languages.

Mel's familiarity with the importance of fly fishing etiquette goes back some twenty-five or thirty years, when he was asked to prepare a lecture on streamside etiquette while working for the Fenwick Fly Fishing Schools. He concluded that "the general concepts of streamside etiquette are mostly rules to be followed, and that these rules vary considerably in different areas and even on individual rivers and lakes. In actuality, what we tried to communicate to students was not so much these varying rules, but simply good manners."

*W*hy do people fish?

The essence of good manners in fishing, as elsewhere, must be predicated on a genuine understanding of other people. Why do our fellow anglers try to connect with these slimy, primitive creatures that live in the water? What motivates people to play our quixotic fishing games? These are questions that every one of us must consider in our encounters with other anglers. In order to really understand other fishers however, we must first understand ourselves. Why *do* we fish?

Just as desserts are the best part of my dinner, the last hour of daylight is my favorite fishing time. I commonly pick out a special pool or run to fish at this time. I redo my leader, put on a fresh fly and approach my chosen spot just as that magic time between light and dark descends. I suspect that only another fisher could fully understand the anticipation of that moment. On one such evening, as I rounded a bend in the river, there, before me, stood some klunk with what appeared to be a surf rod, throwing a huge weight into the middle on MY pool. As I looked down at the waves breaking against the shore, and the satisfied look on this man's face, I hated him. He had no right to be fishing in my pool. He didn't deserve it. He didn't know how to fish properly. He probably was a wife beater. Fortunately, I have mellowed a bit over the years, and in more rational moments, understand that this fork-sticked angler was getting something out of fishing that I often envy. His was a relaxed and comfortable attitude and approach to fishing, whereas mine was more like a small-scale war. Obviously there appear to be differences in the "whys" of fishing.

Roderick Haig-Brown once said, "I still don't know why I fish or why other men fish, except we like it and it makes us think and feel. But I do know that if it were not for the strong, quick life of rivers, for their sparkle in the sunshine, for the cold grayness of them under rain and the feel of them about my legs as I set my feet hard down on the rocks or sand or gravel, I should fish less often. Perhaps fishing is, for me, only an excuse to be near rivers. If so, I'm glad I thought of it."

Yes, there is something wondrous about waters, something wild and mysterious; something sensual and exciting; coming over a hill or around a bend in a river, and seeing and hearing new waters is always stirring. And who among us is not awed by waterfalls?

Why do we fish? I don't think we can discount some sort of inherent need in all of us to gather food, to hunt. It's a simplistic return to Nature.

Fishing can also be an escape, a retreat from the responsibilities and obligations of our everyday lives. We need occasional isolation to help put the various aspects of our lives into their proper perspective.

Competition plays a role in our fishing—not just in tournaments, but for choice positions in crowded waters, for status among other anglers, and even amongst our friends. "Low man on the totem pole buys dinner". . . or "Five bucks in the pot for the biggest fish." And so on.

When I was a young man my uncle often took me fishing in the Gulf of Mexico. Uncle Art was one of my favorite people, but he was extremely competitive. If in a day's fishing he caught two fish and I caught one, the day was beautiful, and all was well with the world. If, however, he caught ten fish and I happened to catch eleven, it was a miserable trip and no one could even talk to him for two days. I suspect there is a little of Uncle Art in all of us.

But fly fishing is also one of the few sports where there need be no competition. In fact, walking a river, hunting for treasures among the shining stones at the waters' edge, contemplating the struggles of an emerging caddis, and even casting your fly with such a comfortable, repetitive rhythm that you secretly hope that no fish will disturb you: that also is a part of fishing. I find that many of my more meaningful moments take place between catches. Tom McGuane calls these times "the long silences," and they too play an important part in why people fish.

Robert Traver, in his classic *Testament of a Fisherman,* said that fishing is "solitude without loneliness." Isn't that beautiful? How true! Fishing is indeed solitude. But it is more. It is also camaraderie. Time on the waters must also include people, because they can be even more beautiful and more intriguing than fish. Sharing your fishing experience with friends can be one of the more satisfying aspects of angling. Perhaps that is why some of us derive so much satisfaction from guiding and teaching.

And loneliness? Yes, even loneliness can be a part of fishing. I remember a dark night on an unknown river feeling very much alone and a bit afraid . . . and scary wading . . . and bears . . . and one time, a bull moose. Afterwards, my fears, and yes, my loneliness, became a delicious memory.

Robert Traver also said he fished because one day "he might catch a mermaid." Think about this marvelous and intriguing concept. Connecting with something unknown, suddenly feeling life through the line in your hands—it could be the biggest fish that ever lived. It might even be a mermaid. There is no doubt that this connection, this sensual contact with something wild and mysterious is a very special part of our fly fishing experience.

Why do we fish? I believe I know why we fish. Fishing is a composite of all of man's moods—mystery, adventure, tranquility, solitude, camaraderie, escape. Fishing is being, is living, is Life. I think we fish because each day we create our own fishing fairy tale; and because there are times we catch—and times we find—ourselves.

Perhaps this little poem I wrote some years ago sums it all up:

> Fairy tales of man and moods and trout
> Of land and waters, care and cause without.
> Quixotic games, the rivers' chuckling sound
> To solitude and love, where self is found.

Part One
HISTORICAL CONTRIBUTIONS

During the course of my historical research on this book, I found it fascinating that the topic of etiquette had indeed been addressed from the very beginning of angling literature. I came across so many well-expressed and varied approaches to the issue at hand that I decided to include an entire section from the past.

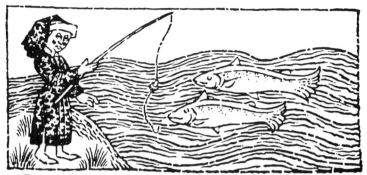

Cratoz quidam pifcabatur Ũnde efcam inhamatam
pifcibus oftendebat turius autem et triutha intuen
tes efcam ipfam plurimũ peroprabãt Bʒ lucius ige-

DAME JULIANA BERNERS
Fifteenth Century

Dame Juliana Berners was a noblewoman versed in the field sports, and prioress of the nunnery at Sopwell, northwest of London. *Treatyse of Fysshynge with an Angle*, attributed to her, appeared in the 1496 edition of *Boke of Saint Albans*, the first sporting book published in the English language. Berners was the first woman to be published in English, and in her contribution, she describes fishing with an artificial fly, the equipment used, and the customs that should be observed.

From *Treatyse of Fysshynge with an Angle*
Boke of Saint Albans, 1496, as found in
The Origins of Angling, by John McDonald
The Lyons Press, 1997

I charge and require you in the name of all noble men that you do not fish in any poor man's private water without his permission and his goodwill. Also, I charge that you break no man's hedges in going about your sports, nor open any man's gates without shutting them again. You must use this sport mainly for your enjoyment or when you intend to go to your amusements in fishing. You will not want very many persons with you who might hinder you in your pastime. Also you must not be too greedy in catching your said game, as in taking too much at one time, for that could easily be the occasion of destroying your own game sport and other men's also. All those that do according to this rule will have the blessing of God and St. Peter.

Ray Bergman
1891-1967

For many years, Bergman was the fishing editor for *Outdoor Life,* and on his watch he saw huge leaps in technology, including spin tackle and monofilament lines. Still, he remained a fisherman first and foremost, and his 1938 publication *Trout* was for many years the only book many anglers ever cared to read or felt they needed to read. It has been called the best fishing book ever written. Until the appearance of Ernest Schwiebert's two-volume *Trout,* Bergman's book held the honor of the largest book ever devoted to a single fish in American publishing. His other titles include *Just Fishing; With Fly, Plug, and Bait;* and *Fresh Water Bass.*

Angling Ethics and Conclusion
From *Just Fishing*, Penn Publishing Co., 1932

$\mathcal{B}$ill Randebrock and I have been inseparable fishing companions for years. Today we feel lost without each other's company. I shall never forget my first day's fishing with Bill. It took place many years ago on a small stream near my home. We had both gone to the brook with different parties and met early in the day. I had picked out a stretch of good water for my guest to fish and had wandered down the road over a mile before breaking into the brook to do my fishing. As I came down to the water I saw Bill fishing. I knew him but slightly then so I said hello and started to withdraw but he stopped me.

"Don't go," said he. "Let's fish down the brook together."

The invitation surprised me. No one had ever suggested doing that before. Everyone I had ever fished with wanted to go it alone and they were never very anxious to give up the better waters either.

"But I don't want to spoil your fishing," I demurred.

"It will be fun to have you," insisted Bill. "The fellow with me didn't seem to like my company and has disappeared and I like to have a comrade to fish with."

And that was the beginning of a friendship which has ever deepened with each succeeding year. It has, in a large measure, taught us tolerance, good sportsmanship and the real meaning of ideal comradeship. One cannot continually share a trout stream with another without becoming better for the sacrifices and the self-denials it entails. I know that I have become a better angler through following this practice. I also know that the lessons learned in following our stream code of ethics has made me a more likable companion to other anglers when I go fishing with them. And it is nice to know that folks enjoy your company and appreciate your courtesy. It gives one far more pleasure than the catching of an extra trout or two which one might have captured had he thought of only himself first.

Angling, if followed in the spirit of contemplative and thoughtful attitude it fosters, is bound to strengthen the character. Because of it I look forward to a beautiful old age, declining years filled with glorious memories. And even when I do get so feeble that I cannot wade a stream I shall have the blessed memories with me until the end.

My wife says that she wonders why all women do not seek anglers for husbands. She has come in contact with many in her life with me and she claims that they all have a sweetness in their nature which others lack. Well, how could one ever spend countless hours following the gentle art, listening to the song of nature, without absorbing some of its atmosphere?

Just fishing! All life is that to some extent. If we are not fishing for one thing it is another. But angling! That's just a bit different. In it we find peace and contentment and much with which to occupy our minds. May the balance of our fishing days be blessed with congenial comrades and "tight lines."

JOE BROOKS
1902-1972

A generation of anglers grew up under the tutelage of Joe Brooks, who served as Fishing Editor for *Outdoor Life* after Ray Bergman vacated that post. Brooks authored numerous books—among them his classic *Trout Fishing*. In his monthly columns, he helped usher in the modern world of fly fishing in both fresh and salt water, and led the way as Americans began to travel widely to fish. His fishing led him to world record tarpon in the Florida Keys with a young captain named Stu Apte, and it put him in company with a Livingston, Montana, tackle shop proprietor named Dan Baily, developing fly patterns for western waters. He is buried on the banks of the Yellowstone River, upstream from Livingston.

Stream Manners and Safety
From *Complete Book of Fly Fishing*, Outdoor Life Books, 1958

*T*he fly fisherman should, and usually does, lead the field in his regard for stream manners. It doesn't take many trips to a trout stream to discover that "Do as you would be done by" is practical as well as polite.

In trout fishing there are certain time-honored rules of behavior and as they are readily applicable to stream fishing, it doesn't take long for the novice to learn them, either from friendly advice or just plain firsthand experience and observation. It stands to reason that a man fishing a dry fly upstream is not going to appreciate seeing another angler step into the same pool above him . . . in other words, cut him off from the pattern he has laid out for fishing that pool.

I remember one occasion when I had inched my way across a treacherous rapid in order to get to the ideal spot from which to cast to a riser I had spotted. I had crept up on him carefully, then stood there motionless for several minutes to let the wave subside, that I had put up with my wading. I wanted everything to be right because this was a big-looking fish.

Then, just as I was about to cast, a fisherman suddenly appeared from the woods at the head of the pool, waved an arm at me and splashed in and started to cast. The trout I had been stalking so carefully pushed up a wave a mile high as he headed for shelter. No one caught any fish out of that pool. Yet if that brash, though friendly fisherman had only stopped to think, both of us might have taken trout. I could have had my try for that big one, and gone on to the next pool, and he could have come in behind me fifteen minutes later and probably caught fish, too.

For it is surprising how quickly trout forget. They have short memories and even when the water is fairly heavily fished, an angler who uses a careful approach can usually make contact with a properly presented fly.

If a second angler must fish that same pool, then he should certainly come in at the lower stretches, the only exception being a very large pool, say 400 feet long, where it is reasonable to go in at the head, even though another angler may be fishing the tail of the pool or the middle, or vice versa. In that long a pool there is usually room for two or three rods.

When moving up or downstream it is always best to walk well back from the banks of the stream so as not to disturb the fish for others.

Another of my bitter memories is of a friend from the East who discovered me on my favorite dry fly river, the Big Hole, in Montana, last summer. I was again working up on a nice trout that was feeding just under an overhanging bank, where the current came around a curve. Suddenly I heard a loud halloo and looked up from the pinpoint spot to which I was casting. There was my friend, waving his arms joyfully, full of good fellowship.

"I've been looking for you all up and down the river," he yelled. "Sure am glad I found you."

I couldn't reciprocate in kind. There he was, standing immediately above that fish, thumping his feet gladly, so that even if the trout had not been able to see him silhouetted against the sky, it could certainly hear him. It was the end of a good day's fishing, and also of a great friendship.

Even when quitting a pool, the angler should move quietly, making as little disturbance as he can, so that the fish will settle as soon as possible, for the next comer.

Of course, it is easier to practice good stream manners in the western part of the country than in the East. Out there the trout streams are more numerous, and there are comparatively few fishermen. But even on crowded eastern waters it shouldn't be necessary to behave as a crowd of anglers did on one occasion I witnessed on Beaver Creek in Maryland.

I was watching a fly caster working his way along a pool, when only five feet from shore he hooked a trout. While he was fighting it, fishermen seemed to appear suddenly from all directions, as if alerted by radio beam. They threw flies over that man's head, under his raised arms. Spoons whizzed past his ears. Everyone seemed to expect to catch fish, just because he had hooked one, when all the while his hooked fish had, of course, stirred up the pool so much that all the other trout were hiding under rocks on the bottom.

Finally one of the over-anxious anglers did whoop: "I've got one!"

What he had was the first fisherman's line, and in the resultant tangle the fly fisherman lost his trout, and again no one got a fish.

Not to discredit my native Maryland, the Maryland State Game and Fish Association was one of the first to post streams with a code of stream manners, and it did plenty of good. With the exception of a few cases such as just described, Maryland stream manners today are something for trout fishermen of other states to strive for. And certainly if sportsmen's groups do not look after such niceties of fishing, then it is up to the State Game and Fish Commissions to do so.

Another important phase of stream manners which all too many of us leave to "the other fellow," is the angler's treatment of the stream he is fishing, and the land around it. The fisherman should regard it as his privilege, not his right, to fish on private property. Permission should always be sought from the owner, and the property should be treated, not as so many are apt to say, "as if it were your own," but rather, definitely as if it were not your own but someone else's and you were there on sufferance. Gates should be carefully closed, field crops treated with respect, and trash should be properly taken care of.

John McDonald, *Fortune Magazine* editor and crack fly fisherman, had a word for some of the sights the fly fisherman comes upon on his trek up a stream—"wilderness slums," he called them, and it's an apt description of the slovenly mess of old tin cans, beer bottles and scraps of paper so often scattered to the winds by careless people who should never be allowed out of a cage. And these are usually the very ones who will wonder why, when next time the farmer says "No" when they want to fish.

Particularly in the western part of the country, the angler should always treat cattle with respect. I know of one ranch in Colorado where anglers booed at, waved at and chased and otherwise disturbed the cattle, which had been gentled in preparation for showing at livestock fairs, until the rancher finally had to post his land. Except in very rare instances, cattle will not annoy the angler, if he does not annoy them. And to be sure, for his own safety, that he is not entering a field with one of those very rare instances, he should obtain the rancher's permission. No rancher will knowingly allow him to go into such a danger spot.

One of the best examples of good farmer-sportsman relations may be seen on 23-mile-long Spring Creek, which runs through Lewistown, Montana. There is not a single "posted" sign along its entire length. Instead there are notices erected by the ranchers, telling anglers where to park their cars, and the ranchers have cleared such parking spots wherever there is an entrance to the river. Not to be outdone by the ranchers, the Lewistown sportsmen, led by Nate Mane and Hash Nelson, have erected stiles over all the fences, in order to prevent damage, and have painted them white so the fishermen can readily see them. That is one stream where everyone, rancher and angler alike, is happy.

Another thing which all fishermen should remember is that the other fellow may be out for his only day astream in the whole year. It doesn't hurt to give him a chance, give him the big end of the bargain, the best part of the pool, tell him what flies you've had luck with that day, where the fish are and where they are hitting. I don't think such everyday politeness has ever cost me a fish, in all my years of fishing. And a little effort on the part of each angler, in that way, will eventually pay off in big dividends in the overall picture of stream etiquette.

While lakes are much wider and roomier than rivers, the same laws of fishing etiquette apply—when a fisherman hooks a fish in a certain spot, other anglers should not immediately crowd over, hampering his fishing, and probably scaring any other fish that may be around. Give him room—and take room for yourself.

Even with a whole ocean to fish in, I have seen some horrible things happen in the salt. One time I was knee deep on a Key Largo, Florida, flat, stalking a particularly large bonefish that was tailing up a fit in his search for food. The very way he was working showed that he was hungry, and I felt that my chances were good if I could just get close enough to put the fly in front of him. For 100 feet I sneaked along, putting each foot down carefully, so as not to make a noise in the water, or grind coral rock beneath my feet. Then I was ready. He was just 50 feet away from me, his tail still waving in the sunlight, quite unaware of any danger. I got my fly in the air, started the back-cast—but I never completed it. Just at that moment a skiff hit the edge of the flat, with motor going full blast. Within seconds the bonefish was pushing a big wave in front of him as he sped for the deep.

A few minutes later, when that carefree outboarder asked me if I was catching anything, I couldn't even answer. He probably thought that I was dumb. It's all right with me, I think he was dumb, in a different way.

Any fisherman who has fished at all, or read about fishing, should know better than to roar into shallow water with a motor going full blast, and not expect to spook fish. And it's twice as bad to spook them for the other fellow as for himself.

This business of motors in shallow water has become so serious in the salt that there's a whole tribe of fishermen who probably don't know that to the fly fisherman (or other casting enthusiast) they are known as "barracuda people," as if they were little men from outer space, scarcely human. These are the boys who troll through water so shallow that they are always either dredging the bottom with the propeller or hooking up their trolling outfits on rocks and weeds. They catch barracuda —sure—but if they would move out beyond the edge of the flats, where the water is a little deeper, they would catch more barracuda and bigger barracuda, would not run all the bonefish out of the shallows, and then light tackle anglers would be able to enjoy their sport, too.

Similarly, when anglers are trolling, either in fresh or salt water, and see a caster working the shoreline, they should give him a wide berth. The caster does not cover nearly so much ground as the troller, and therefore should be entitled to at least a polite amount of room around him, in which to wave his rod.

Etiquette Among Fishermen
From *Tricks and Knacks of Fishing,* published
by Horton Mfg. Co., 1911

*T*here are certain unwritten laws of courtesy which prevail among fishermen. The amateur who doesn't know them, or the angler who disregards them, will soon become unpopular with his fellows.

It is bad etiquette for an angler in a boat to cross another fisherman's trolling line, or even follow a boat close enough to be over or in the immediate vicinity of a trolling bait.

It is bad etiquette to pass another boat so close that the oars almost touch.

It is bad etiquette fly casting on stream or lake to trespass on the surface close to another caster, or to cut in ahead of him on brook or shore line in order to find unwhipped water.

It is bad etiquette in plug or still fishing to anchor your boat close to another boat merely because it is having luck and you are not.

It is bad etiquette to treat a brother angler, even though you never saw him before, in any other than a courteous and gentlemanly manner.

P. Allen Parsons

"P. A." had fished since early childhood in Massachusetts, and had an encyclopedic knowledge of fish. He was renowned among the outdoor experts of his day, and in the early days of fly fishing, he made sporting history by proving that saltwater fish would hit dry flies! After retiring from a lifelong career in advertising, he joined *Outdoor Life*, where he remained for over twenty-five years.

The Fisherman's Ethics

From *Complete Book of Fresh Water Fishing,*
Outdoor Life Books, Harper & Row, 1963

*S*tates and provinces set up laws regulating fishing seasons, creel limits, size limits, and methods of taking. Their object is to provide better fishing for all. But the individual conduct of the fisherman is largely a matter of conscience and decency and not of regulation by law. All those who hunt and fish are mistakenly called "sportsmen" in the public prints, though many of them do not deserve the title. The true sportsman consciously or instinctively follows the

Golden Rule—"Do unto others as you would have them do unto you."

The sportsman obeys the fishing laws to the letter. He knows they were drawn up by trained men, better versed in conditions than he, and are designed not to hurt his sport but to better it.

If it is necessary to cross private lands in order to reach a stream or lake, or to fish on private property, the sportsman asks permission from the owner. When crossing privately owned lands, he does not walk over seeded fields or go through uncut hay lands, but follows a fence line where he will do no damage. Should he come to a closed gate, he closes it after him; if the gate is open, he leaves it open. He does not drive over private lands without permission, and then drives only where told he may.

He does not build a fire without permission, and then only where he can build it on mineral soil, using extreme care to remove any combustible materials to a safe distance from the site. Before leaving he douses the fire, stirring the ashes with a stick so that every ember is wet and safe. If a smoker, he does not throw away a lighted cigarette or cigar without being sure that it is out. He will use the same caution with a pipe.

He leaves no litter anywhere he goes. Any tin can or bottle is buried, the tin cans flattened by stamping on them. Paper, even the wrapper of a candy bar, is either burned safely or stuffed into his pockets to carry home with him. He is orderly in all his acts.

He cuts down a tree only with permission. He does not dig up any plant or shrub without permission. He does not camp without permission, and having had it, leaves the campsite clean. On leaving the property he thanks the owner for the privilege that was given him.

The real sportsman conducts himself toward other fishermen just as properly. If he is fishing a stream and comes upon another angler fishing a pool or stretch of water, he goes around him, walking well back from the bank, knowing that the sight of him would alarm the fish and curtail the fellow angler's sport. He throws no trash, caps, or bottles into the water to pollute it or possibly cut the waders of another angler.

If driving a motor-powered boat on a lake or pond, he keeps well away from the anchored boat of another fisherman and cuts down his speed. A high-powered motor boat can set up waves that are a hazard to small boats and may even swamp them. The great increase in the use of motor boats, and the recklessness of their drivers, have blown up a storm among fishermen who have demanded that the authorities exercise greater supervision over them.

This sportsman, should he/she fish with you, is modest. He does not boast of his catch, commends you on your casting, and is happy if you creel a good fish. When you come to a fine, fishy-looking stretch of water, he's likely to tell you, "There should be a good fish there. Go ahead and try it. I'll move along a little way." If he puts on a fly that gets fish, and you haven't that pattern, he insists on your taking one or two from his box.

Following these unwritten laws of good conduct is sure to earn a fisherman respect and admiration; it is not strange that such anglers not only add to the pleasure of others but that they themselves get the utmost out of the sport.

JAMES QUICK
d. 1960

Jim Quick, of Santa Monica, California, was a promotional writer and lecturer for the aircraft and petroleum industries. After World War II, he cofounded a select fishing tackle corporation, and in his latter years gave expert advice to sportsmen on angling instruction and tackle selection. In addition to being a cartoonist and artist, he wrote *Trout Fishing and Trout Flies* and *Fishing the Nymph*.

Sportsmen's Ethics
From *Trout Fishing and Trout Flies*, Countryman Press, 1957, by arrangement with A. S. Barnes Co., Inc.

*W*hether called formality, good form, civility, etiquette, manners, courtesy, or ethics, one could fill a modest volume on things one should or shouldn't do in the opinion of real sportsmen if one wished to be regarded, himself, as a sportsman or just a real man on the stream.

I could plead that you do not walk up to the bank's edge if another fisherman is working in that spot. I could suggest that the fisherman working downstream, and meeting another angler fishing upstream, leave the water and circle around at a suitable distance before re-entering the water.

The same procedure would be applicable if fishing from the bank or the stream's edge. I could advise that a fisherman wading the water and coming up on another angler fishing a particular hole, either from the bank or wading himself, wait until he is finished or get out and go around. I could urge one, if having fished a pool or a good pocket for a reasonable length of time, with others patiently waiting for a crack at it also, to pass on up- or down-stream, at least temporarily, until they move on leaving the spot open for one to go back. However, I won't admonish you on any particular situation but will cover it in one sweeping Golden Rule plea:

Treat the other angler, as you, in any situation, would want to be treated.

If you are a cantankerous, obstinate, self-willed individual who feels you should, for any or no reason, be given preferred exemption and you won't, by gosh, give an inch, you have no business or right on a trout stream. The Creator gave us a heavenly privilege of fishing trout and he who deliberately cheats or purposely acts contrary to accepted sportsmanship practices should be toted on a knotty rail three times around the earth at the equator and I'll furnish the tar!

Robert Scharff, Editor

Etiquette for Fishermen
From *Esquire's Book of Fishing*, Harper & Row, 1962

The best gauge of one fisherman's consideration for another is the space he gives him. The unwritten law of lake and stream is: "Finders keepers." Whichever fisherman got there first has prior rights to all fish within reasonable casting distance.

This means not only that you must give him at least 75 feet

Combat fishing.

clearance on all sides, but also that you must avoid disturbing the water in his area and, regardless of the peace and space you allow him, avoid picking off fish on their way to his chosen spot.

If you and the man who got there fastest are in some wilderness not yet discovered by the nation's other 21,419,978 licensed fishermen, follow the old rule: one rod to a stream. But if you're fishing an area where you can't possibly put other fishermen out of sight, mind these don'ts, at least:

Don't cast across the water being fished by another angler.

Don't wade through a pool being fished by another. If you encounter another fisherman while you're stream fishing, detour around him.

Don't cast into the mouth of a small feeder stream on a lake if another man is already fishing the feeder.

Don't let your boat disturb the waters near another fisherman. Above all, don't run your outboard close astern to a trolling boat.

When you want to fish private waters, by all means get prior permission. Permission will seldom be refused—in fact, navigable streams and state-stocked ponds are not legally private, regardless of houses built on their shores, but the courtesy of your request will smooth the waters.

As a fisherman's guest, you supply nothing but your own equipment except by prior arrangement. Your host takes care of lunch and all expenses. (At a club, the expenses include pound or unit prices for every fish you take, so guard your greed—and realize that "your" fish belong to your host!) He won't, however, expect to supply you with fishing equipment, so get it straight at the outset what clothes and tackle you'll need. As one outdoor editor once put it:

"There are three things—maybe four—that no man will lend to another: his dog, his fishing rod, his gun—and possibly, his wife."

Practical considerations, not etiquette, govern the clothes that you fish in.

The fish can't see colors or hear rustles; fishermen can't object to the most battered talisman hat. Fishermen's wives and club officers may have their own objections to muddy boots and fishy jackets, however, so you will need a change of clothes whenever you expect to wind up at a table instead of at a camp site.

Your guide on a fishing trip is not a servant, to be bossed about, nor a country cousin, to be patronized. Treat him like a somewhat senior fishing companion—with respect. Call him "Mr." if he was introduced that way, until he decides to favor you with his first name. Better not drop names and fish stories in his direction; he'll be impressed only by performance. And when you tip him at trip's end at the rate of $2 to $5 a day give him the money as his due, not as if you were bestowing a favor.

In the matter of conservation, official limits are unreliable guides to how many fish you may acceptably take home. The limits set by game laws or club rules are maximums, seldom approached by the conscientious sportsman. The purist often goes home empty-handed as a matter of principle rather than luck. His sport has been to fish, not to dispense his catch to the neighbors. Without question, he puts back every fish he does not need. And in the rare fishing ground where by-laws prevent his returning a fish he has caught to the water (a few clubs operate on the theory that a hooked fish is a hurt fish and should not be put back) he may cut short his day's sport rather than catch more fish than he has immediate, personal use for.

A bulging creel is suspect on another score. The avid angler, who can foresee the day when he won't know where his next fish is coming from, deplores the kind of tackle which makes it easy for the unskilled to haul in fish. Particularly if you are using unconventional or "foolproof" tackle, travel light on the way home.

And you might as well fish with trap and net as turn up with a spinner or a worm among dry-fly trout fishermen. A polite fisherman will take pains never to ridicule your tackle or your methods. He will pretend to believe that anything goes, and that the "right" way is any way that catches fish. He may even apologize for his own "eccentric" adherence to old-fashioned techniques. But it's all an act of good manners! So when you're new, when you're a guest, and when you care about the opinion of others, play it safe. Use the tackle and lures your host suggests. Inquire about club ground rules or customs, then fish up to them without comment. And whenever you're in doubt, do it "the hard way."

———⚬⚬⚬———

Samuel R. Slaymaker II

A graduate of Cambridge University in England, Samuel R. Slaymaker II later joined the Slaymaker Lock Company, where he became executive vice president, advertising and public relations manager, and secretary. He developed several fly patterns, the most famous being the "Little Brown Trout." In 1968 he received the "Order of the Hat" from the Fly Fishing Club of Harrisburg, Pennsylvania, for his work on trout conservation. He published articles in many magazines including *Sports Afield*, *Outdoor Life*, and *Esquire*.

Ten Commandments of Stream Etiquette
From *Simplified Fly Fishing*, Harper & Row, 1969

*I*mplicit in a civilization's development is increasing awareness of manners. This is especially true in sports, whether the competition is between man and man or man and animal. In the latter case fox hunting, for example, dictates of good form sometimes become extremely complicated but surprisingly, rules of etiquette are not generally equated with angling. This will probably continue to be the case until angling is defined as a pastime rather than a sport, for sport connotes competition, and fishing is more than just a contest in killing fish. When more anglers become less obsessed with competing against each other and concentrate more on matching wits with their quarry, angling etiquette may evolve more rapidly. This will bode well for the future of the ancient and honorable tradition of fly fishing.

Even in the most exalted angling circles you will hear references to someone "out-fishing" someone else. This is unfortunate, for anglers absorbed solely in outwitting their quarry become skillful faster, and very quickly their self-confidence precludes competing with other fishermen.

So the *First Commandment* of angling etiquette should be to compete with fish, not other anglers.

The *Second Commandment* hinges on the first: only kill fish (particularly trout) when there is good reason to do so.

Conservation organizations emblazon streamside trees with posters reminding anglers that they'll catch more fish if they kill less. "Catch and Release" stretches are dedicated to this proposition. I suggested in the Introduction, dwindling trout habitats and burgeoning numbers of fishermen dictate the need for the adoption of the "catch and release" philosophy by all who fish for trout with flies. The urgings of interested organizations in the name of conservation will help, but real progress won't be made until the killing of trout as a yardstick of success is considered a breach of angling etiquette.

There are times when exceptions to the rule can, and in some cases should, be made. Deeply hooked fish are often unharmed when the leader is snipped and the fish is released with the hook still embedded. His enzymes will eventually rot out the hook. But if a fish bleeds profusely, chances are it will die, so it might as well be creeled. When you're fortunate enough to land a trophy trout (one in the 18- or 20-inch range) you should feel free to kill it, for such trout sometimes become cannibalistic and prey on smaller populations. Also, a really big trout can be considered the ultimate in success, so an angler deserves to keep him. When you're camping in a wilderness area with myriads of wild fish, some for the skillet can be condoned, and a few nice trout for a host with whom you're staying, or for a gourmet friend, are perfectly in order. It is this angler's opinion that a person who measures the success of his outing by the weight of his creel is, at best, unenlightened.

It was noted that there is a connection between competing and fish killing. The beginning fly angler sometimes kills fish to prove to his companions—or those at home—that he actually can catch fish. This is only human. Most, if not all of us, who cast flies for trout have gone through this stage, and sometimes it's hard to get out of it.

My father, whose fishing experiences encompassed his boyhood (worms and sunfish), harbors secret misgivings about my fly-fishing abilities. I can tell from the slightly quizzical, half-peeved look that often follows my rejoinder, "released 'em," to his invariable request for "a few trout," on my returns from outings. I've tried to lay low his disbelief, and now and again I do produce a few.

Chances are good that you will come to greatly value fishing for enjoyment rather than meat. You will have become part of a fraternity that elevates the catching of fish to an art form; one with unparalleled literature and tradition which you are helping to preserve by releasing your catches. You should be proud, too, in enabling the hope of our patron saint, Theodore Gordon, to become a reality. Almost a half century ago in describing a stream restricted to flies (an oddity then) he wrote, "Such a law as this would be of great benefit to all trout streams . . . ."

As Charles K. Fox says in his *Rising Trout,* "Theodore Gordon fathered and championed the concept of fishing for sport as opposed to meat. He sold to many the idea of putting them back alive, something the English weren't doing."

The *Third Commandment* of stream etiquette proscribes "horning in."

Often it's unintentional, but anglers should guard against moving into water soon to be fished by someone already on-stream. Scout the area for others. Either fish behind another party or get well ahead. When the next man reaches your starting point, sufficient time should have elapsed to permit the fish to settle down.

Commandment Four follows logically: cut your wading to a minimum. Only do so to facilitate casting. When possible, use dry rocks as steppingstones. You won't disturb water for those behind, and you'll be easier on subsurface fly larvae.

Commandment Five contributes to optimum enjoyment when you're fishing with a companion. Give him the opportunity to fish alone. He might find you charming company, but he might also enjoy solitary communion with the stream. If he wants to stay with you, give him equal opportunity to fish the best spots. This is easily accomplished by taking turns by the stretch. As you move along a stream the hot spots tend to even out between you.

Excitement often results in an angler's breaking *Commandment Six*. When action is heavy at a given spot, it's easy to spend a lot of time fishing it. Of course, if no one is waiting, stay on, but it's not good form to hog good water when others are on the stream.

Also, if you're fishing in front of another angler, it's best to take no more than a couple of fish from one pool (or distin-guishable spot). It might be that there are only a few fish in that area. A trout that's felt the hook can be fly-shy for days. Judgment must be used, however; if a pool is large, a couple more might be snagged without putting down the majority of fish in it.

But *Commandment Seven*, two fish to a pool, is a good rule of thumb to stick to.

Spinning gear has its places, but one of them is not a proper trout stream. When one fine stream, previously restricted to fly gear, was opened to spinning, it was speedily denuded of native trout. Spinning is that deadly, so it's outlawed on most good club streams. One, on which I've fished in the Poconos, is so anxious to preserve its stream-bred browns that anyone caught with spinning tackle is drummed out and never allowed to return—be he a member or a guest. So *Commandment Eight* calls for fly rods on trout streams.

Commandment Nine will seem so obvious as to preclude mention, but many who should know better sometimes break it through thoughtlessness. Don't litter a trout stream. Nothing mars the beauty of an arbored mountain stream more than cast-off food wrappers, bottles, and cans.

Last summer I was shooting action pictures with Ed Murphy, senior editor of *Sports Afield*, on a gem of a Pocono Mountain stream. Under a hemlock overhanging a beaver pool, Ed's dry Cahill was gobbled by a 14-inch stream-bred brown trout. I had little time to check the area prior to shooting the spectacular action. We noticed the beer can only after Ed's fish was netted and hoped fervently that it wouldn't show. But on each color transparency the half-sunken can, hard against a gnarled root of the hemlock, was jarringly obvious.

Commandment Ten is automatically acknowledged by those of good breeding—the first time. I suggest that it be adhered to repeatedly. When an appreciative angler is permitted to fish private water, he usually offers something to the owner by way of appreciation. Often, though, hospitality is taken for granted by the recipient and appreciative gestures fall away with the years. I'm one of the few guests permitted to fish a native brook trout stream in the Poconos simply because I sent a box of chocolates for the Christmas following my first visit and continued doing so for fifteen years.

By honoring these Ten Commandments of stream etiquette you will increase your enjoyment astream and your companion's and serve to perpetuate the pastime, through your practice of trout conservation and by the example you set for others. You will become a better angler; indeed a better person . . . one with whom the shades of bygone giants like Walton and Cotton, Maryatt and Halford, Hewitt and La Branche could enjoy a summer evening.

Part Two

MODERN SENSIBILITY

As fly fishing grows in popularity, our burgeoning demand for a quality outdoor experience places increased pressure on waters that *don't* get bigger to accommodate all of us. As a result, we find ourselves in crowds and with potentials for conflict far in excess of what our thoughtful and instructive forebears could have envisioned. Their genteel reprimands and admonitions can scarcely address the genuine levels of stress that sometimes accompany a day astream. Civility rather than solitude becomes the gauge of a day.

As pressure on the resource increases, we find that respect for the fish and the water they live in becomes critical. Etiquette extends itself to a respect for the natural environment and a conservation ethic as we seek not only to continue to enjoy our sport, but also to maintain and preserve it for the future.

Roderick Haig-Brown
1908-1976

Roderick Haig-Brown was a writer, a conservationist with an international reputation, a judge, and a university chancellor. He and his wife, Ann, settled on the bank of the Campbell River on northern Vancouver Island in 1934. Haig-Brown's published work includes 25 books and well over 200 articles and speeches. Best known for his essays on fly fishing, rivers, conservation, and family life, Haig-Brown is now recognized as an increasingly prescient voice concerning the social and environmental conditions of the Pacific West Coast in particular, and the larger world in general. His best known works include *A River Never Sleeps*, *The Western Angler*, and *Return to the River*. In addition to his work as an essayist, Haig-Brown wrote two adult novels and several novels for young people. He also served as a member of three Federal Electoral Boundary Commissions and the International Pacific Salmon Commission.

Articles of Faith for Good Anglers
1960

Some twenty million angling licenses a year are sold on the North American continent and considerably more than twenty million people go fishing each year. There isn't a reason in the world to suppose that twenty million people really enjoy going fishing; a remarkably high proportion of them contribute vastly to the discomfort of others while finding little joy in the sport for themselves. This is sad but inevitable; it grows directly out of the misconception that anyone with two hands, a hook, and a pole, is equipped to go fishing.

Fishing is not really a simpleton's sport. It is a sport with a long history, an intricate tradition, and a great literature. These things have not grown by accident. They have developed by the devotion of sensitive and intelligent men and they make not only a foundation for rich and satisfying experience but the charter of a brotherhood that reaches around the world and through both hemispheres.

It is a brotherhood well worth joining. There are no papers to sign, no fees to pay, no formal initiation rites. All that is required is some little understanding of the sport itself and a decent respect for the several essentials that make it.

The first purpose of going fishing is to catch fish. But right there the angler separates himself from the meat fisherman and begins to set conditions. He fishes with a rod and line and hook—not with nets or traps or dynamite. The fisherman is seeking to catch fish on his own terms, terms that will yield him the greatest sense of achievement and the closest identification with his quarry.

This establishes the first unwritten article of the brotherhood. Fishing is a sport, a matter of intimate concern only to fish and fisherman; it is not a competition between man and man. The man's aim is to solve by his own wits and skill the unreasoning reaction of the fish, always within the limits of his self-imposed conditions. The fisherman is his own referee, umpire, steward, and sole judge of his performance.

Completely alone, by remote lake or virgin stream, he remains bound by his private conditions and the vagaries of fish and weather. Within those conditions, he may bring all his ingenuity to bear, but if he departs from them or betrays them,

Not so peaceful, even back then! (New Jersey, 1927)

though only God and the fish are his witnesses, he inevitably reduces his reward.

This total freedom from competitive pressure leads the fisherman directly to the three articles of faith that really govern the brotherhood: respect for the fish, respect for the fish's living space, and respect for other fishermen. All three are interrelated and, under the crowded conditions of today's fishing waters, all three are equally important.

Respect for other fishermen is simply a matter of common courtesy and reasonably good manners. The more crowded the waters the more necessary manners become and the more thoroughly they are forgotten. The rule can be expressed in a single golden-rule phrase: "Give the other guy the kind of break you would like to get for yourself." Don't crowd him, don't block him, don't push him. If he is working upstream, don't cut in above him; if he is working downstream, don't pile in directly below him. If you see he is hooking fish along some favorite weed bed, don't force your boat in beside him and spoil it for both. Don't park all day in what you think is a favored spot so that no one else can get near it—give it a fair try and move on.

On uncrowded waters a self-respecting fisherman always gives the other fellow first chance through the pool or the drift; as often as not the second time through is just as good. On crowded waters give whatever room and show whatever consideration you can and still wet a line; better still, try somewhere else. The crowds are usually in the wrong places anyway.

If you would be part of the brotherhood, be generous. Don't hide the successful fly or lure or bait; explain every last detail of it and give or lend a sample if you can. Show the next man along where you moved and missed the big one, make him aware of whatever little secret you may have of the river's pools or the lake's shoals or the sea's tides—but only if the other guy wants it. If he doesn't, be generous still and keep quiet. If he wants to tell you his secret instead of listening to yours, reach for your ultimate generosity and hear him out as long as you can stand it. Good things sometimes come from unlikely sources.

Respect for the fish is the real base of the whole business. He is not an enemy, merely an adversary, and without him and his progeny there can be no sport. Whatever his type and species, he has certain qualities that make for sport and he must be given a chance to show them to best advantage. He is entitled to the consideration of the lightest gear and the subtlest method the angler can use with a reasonable chance of success. If it takes a little time to learn such skills, there is no doubt the fish is worthy of them. And if the angler is any kind of a man he is unlikely to be satisfied with less.

Even in the moment of success and triumph, when the hooked fish is safely brought to beach or net, he is still entitled to respect and consideration: to quick and merciful death if he is wanted, to swift and gentle release if he is not.

Killing fish is not difficult—a sharp rap on the back of the head settles most species. Releasing fish is a little, but only a little, more complicated. Fly-caught trout of moderate size are easy. Slide the hand down the leader with the fish still in the water, grip the shank of the hook, and twist sharply. Where it is necessary to handle the fish, a thumb and finger grip on the lower jaw does the least harm and is usually effective.

Larger fish that have fought hard are often in distress when released and need to be nursed in the water until they can swim away on their own. Generally little more is needed than to hold them on an even keel, facing upstream, while they take a few gulps of water through their gills. Fish that have bled heavily or fish that have just swum in from salt water are less likely to recover and should be kept.

Respect for the fish's living space should be comprehensive. It includes the water, the bed of the stream or lake, the land on both sides of the water, and all the life that grows there, bird or mammal, plant or fish or insect. There isn't an excuse in the world for litter-leavers, tree-carvers, brush-cutters, flower-pickers, nest-robbers, or any other self-centered vandals on fishing waters. The fisherman comes at best to do some damage—to the fish—and the best he can do is keep it to that. He doesn't need to junk-heap the place with cartons and bottles and tin cans; he need not drop even so much as a leader case or cigarette pack; he can afford to remember that no one else wants to be reminded of him by his leavings.

These are elementary and negative points and if parents raised their children properly there would be no need to mention them in this context. A fisherman, any kind of a fisherman, should know better than to spoil the place that makes his sport. But a true share in the brotherhood calls for a little more. The fisherman is under obligation to learn and understand something about the life of his fish and the conditions it needs, if only so that he can take his little part in helping to protect them.

All fish need clean waters and all nations, if they know what is good for them, can afford to keep their waters clean. Pollution, whether from sewage or industrial wastes, starts as a little thing scarcely noticed and goes on to destroy all the life of the waters. Its damage can be repaired, slowly, painfully, expensively, but there is no excuse for it in the first place, though many are forthcoming.

Besides clean water for their own lives and the many living things they depend on, fish need special conditions for spawning and hatching and rearing. Migratory fish need free passage upstream and down. These things and many others like them are worth understanding not merely because they suggest protections and improvements, but because knowledge of them brings the fisherman closer to the identification he seeks, makes him more truly a part of the world he is trying to share.

The old days and the old ways, when every stream was full of fish and empty of people, are long gone. They weren't as good as they sounded anyway. It took time and the efforts of good fishermen to learn what could be done and should be done to produce the best possible sport. North American angling has now come close to full development. No one is going to get what he should from the sport by simply buying some gear and going out on the water, nor can he achieve very much by sneering at better men than himself who do take the trouble to learn the delicate skills of the subtler methods. The real world of fishing is open to anyone, through the literature and the generosity of the brotherhood. Once entered upon, the possibilities are limitless. But even the casual, occasional fisherman owes the sport some measure of understanding—enough, shall we say, to protect himself and others from the waste and aggravations of discourtesy and bad manners that are so often based on ignorance.

In Winchester Cathedral, not far from a famous trout stream in Hampshire, England, is the tomb of William of Wykeham, a great fourteenth-century bishop and statesman who left a motto to a school he founded: "Manners makyth man." Within the same cathedral lie the bones of our father, Izaak Walton, who remarked three hundred years ago: "Angling is somewhat like poetry, men are to be born so."

Perhaps Izaak's precept is for the inner circle of the brotherhood, but William's is certainly universal. It is just possible that nice guys don't catch the most fish. But they find far more pleasure in those they do get.

⎯⎯⎯⎯ ∞ ⎯⎯⎯⎯

ERNEST SCHWIEBERT

Princeton, New Jersey

Even people who don't fly fish often know the phrase "matching the hatch," and we have Schwiebert to thank for that. *Matching the Hatch* was the title of his first book, a milestone publication, which he wrote and illustrated when he was scarcely in his twenties. Since then there have been few anglers to match his erudition, breadth of experience on the trout and salmon waters of the world, and contributions to the study of aquatic insects and their imitation. Along the way he has written prolifically, with *Salmon of the World,* the two-volume *Trout,* and *Nymphs* headlining his inimitable literary output. A generation of anglers came of age under the influence of Schwiebert, and there are few to match the impact he has had on late-twentieth-century fly fishing.

Ethics, Manners, and Philosophy Astream
From *Trout,* E. P. Dutton, 1978

The Rules of Fishing Etiquette are Logical and Simple.

$\mathcal{N}$oisy wading or wading into the principal holding lies of a pool is always poor manners, even when no one else is fishing there. It will disturb the trout more thoroughly than the normal passage of fishing the pool, which is thoughtless and unfair to the next angler. Wading should always be patient and

Wade quietly, unlike this splashy fellow.

slow, both from consideration for others and because it will produce better results in your own fishing.

Experienced anglers will often study a pool instead of fishing it blindly, and sometimes it is good practice to stop fishing and rest a pool for a few minutes. Such a fisherman has first priority on the pool he is studying or resting, and you should never start fishing without his permission. Most good anglers are courteous and generous toward others, and will even grant their permission to fish a pool they have been resting, if you have the good manners to stop where they are sitting and ask.

Traditionally, the dry fly fisherman wading upstream has the right of way over a wet fly man working down. It is a tradition

Resting the fish—and the angler.

One of the major causes of confrontation: cutting too close in front of another angler.

that makes sense. Fishermen wading upstream are forced by the current to move slowly, cover far less water, and approach the trout from behind. Fish always face the currents and will see an angler fishing downstream more readily. His technique both covers and disturbs more water. The man working down with a wet fly or streamer should retire from the river and move unobtrusively around an angler fishing upstream.

Generosity along the stream extends itself to other things as well. There was a boyhood evening many years ago when I was casting over a big smooth flowing reach of the Madison in the Yellowstone, and a man fishing across the river was catching fish regularly. There were a number of good fish working on my side of the river, but I had failed to touch them for more than an hour.

What're they taking? I finally asked in desperation.

Whitcraft! came the reply.

It was an unfamiliar fly pattern in those boyhood days, and when he caught two more fish I finally swallowed my pride.

What's a Whitcraft? I yelled back curiously.

Take it! The fisherman cast his fly past me and the leader drifted down against my legs.

I picked it up. *Can't do that,* I protested feebly.

Cut it off the tippet, he insisted. *Wouldn't have cast it over if I didn't mean for you to have it!*

Thanks! I clinched it to my tippet.

It was a fine evening, and we both took fish regularly in the one hundred yards of perfect dry fly water. It was a lesson in generosity I have never forgotten, and I always try to give a taking fly to another fisherman if I have an extra pattern or two. Sometimes I have given my only taking fly to a stranger when I have already caught enough fish to satisfy me. It is a good rule to remember on any river.

———

There is also a code governing the final landing of a good fish.

Spectators should keep well back and stay as motionless as possible to keep from frightening the hooked fish and prolonging its struggles.

Several years ago I watched a good fly fisherman playing a big brown in the straw-colored Nez Perce meadows of the Firehole. It was a fish of five or six pounds, hooked on a tiny dry fly with a cobweb-fine leader in a mirror-smooth flat. The fish had been patiently beaten, and it floundered weakly on the surface, but it still had enough strength to hang well out in the main current. The fisherman played it gingerly, managing his fragile tippet with cunning and skill, and the fish was about ready to surrender.

Best fish I've ever hooked, the fisherman said quietly when I stopped to watch. *It should go five or six pounds!*

Beautiful fish, I agreed.

Took a tiny twenty two Adams, the man continued proudly.

Tied it myself over to Madison Campground last night!

They like small flies on the Firehole, I said.

It's been some fight, the fisherman sighed happily. *It's only a 6x tippet and those weeds kept me worried!*

Pretty fine leader, I nodded in agreement.

The fish was finally coming now, circling weakly in the shallows, when a tourist car with Nebraska plates turned off the highway to the Fountain Freight Road in a cloud of dust and gravel. It roared off the road and rocked to a stop near the river, disgorging a man and a large covey of noisy children.

Look there! the man yelled. *He's got one!*

The grassy bank swarmed with children, and the big trout surged back toward midstream in terror. The fisherman looked at me and rolled his eyes in despair.

Hey mister! the father cackled with a false men's club friendliness. *What'd you use for bait?*

Dry fly, said the fisherman unhappily.

Big fish like that don't want no flies, the man laughed to his chattering children. *You need doughballs or nightwalkers.*

How 'bout cheese, screeched one of his older boys.

Good bait too! the man agreed.

It was a nightmare for the fisherman. His face was flushed with anger, but he said nothing and patiently worked the big fish back from the swift currents downstream. The children were throwing pebbles at each other now, racing around through the coarse-grass meadows, and a stone splashed into the shallows near the trout. It bolted back into the heavy currents at midstream. The angler groaned and patiently coaxed it into the shallows again.

Come on! I said to the tourists finally. *Corral your kids and keep them back from the bank!*

You own the river? the man said belligerently.

No, I said, *but all this yelling and running around isn't fair to this man—he could lose his big fish!*

The angler looked at me gratefully.

Hell! one of the children yelled at me, *that fish ain't big—you should see the carp we catch!*

Why don't you pull it in? the man asked.

The angler said nothing and worked the trout into the shallows along the bank. Its strength was spent now, and the fisherman was looking for a gravel bar to beach it when his nightmare reached its frustrating climax.

Here, mister! the man said helpfully and scuttled down the bank. *Let me give you a hand!*

Don't touch the leader! the angler screamed.

But the man ignored him and started hand-lining the fish toward the gravel. *You got him, daddy!* shrieked a pig-tailed little girl. *You got him!*

It was too much for the exhausted trout. It gathered its remaining strength into a final wrenching splash that sheared the fragile nylon like a cobweb and it was gone.

Hey mister, the girl said. *Your string broke!*

The helpless fisherman stared at her wordlessly, and finally he waded out of the shallows toward his car, shaking his head in despair as he passed me. His eyes were glazed with shock. The other man herded his children back into their car.

Can't catch fish with line that weak, I heard him tell his wife, who looked like a Martian with her hair full of plastic rollers.

It was an incident filled with almost bizarre exaggerations, but it has lessons for all anglers. You should never interfere with another fisherman who is into a fish, and you should never offer to net or gaff a fish for another angler unless he asks you. There is an unwritten rule among skilled fly fishermen, particularly those who fish for trout and salmon, that landing a fish yourself is both the moment critique of our fishing and a gesture of homage to its beauty and sporting character. Helping net or gaff a fish for a stranger is always perilous, since the fish may escape in the final moments, and you will always be blamed, however wordlessly. Never assist another fisherman in landing his fish unless you are asked, and even if you are asked, decline unless you are really skilled and experienced. Remember that a fisherman who does not request your help is not necessarily selfish or unfriendly but playing a part in a tradition that believes a big trout or salmon is a quarry with almost mystical qualities, and deserves to meet its fate in a hand-to-hand struggle.

———

You ain't letting that fish go! The man came angrily into the stream. *You're giving it to me!*

No, I said quietly. *It's going back.*

The trout was frightened when the fisherman splashed toward me, and it fought free of my fingers. It held a moment below my waders and darted nervously upstream into the deep smooth flowing throat of the pool where it was safe. The man stood in a rage, spluttering with anger and frustration.

Goddammit, he shouted, *it ain't fair for you fancy pants fly boys to fish and let your fish go when a man like me ain't caught a trout all morning!*

I'm sorry about that, I said, *but a man has to catch his own trout, then you can decide to kill them or let them go.*

What's wrong with my gear? he asked.

It was a heavy spinning rod with a monofilament of about twenty pound breaking strain on its reel. There were several split shot on the nylon, and a nightcrawler was laced on a big bait hook. It was pretty coarse tackle for hard-fished water.

The fish can see your nylon, I said, *and that's an awful lot of lead for a small stream like this one.*

You mean the trout are that smart?

Smart is the one thing trout really are, I smiled. *You have to sneak up on them like a deer or wild turkey.*

Well I'll be damned, he said.

You mean you haven't been concealing yourself from the fish? I asked. *You let them see you before you start fishing?*

Afraid so, he admitted.

Look, I said, *you get yourself some small hooks and a four-pound leader and use less split shot ... sneak up on the pools and get your bait into the water quietly.*

You think that'll help catch fish? he asked.

It should. I nodded my head.

Thanks, the man extended his hand. *If it works out, I might even try some of them flies sometime.*

Good luck! I laughed.

It was an incredible episode, and there were moments when I thought I had a fight on my hands, but it codifies a whole galaxy of problems about trout fishing in our time. The streams and lakes and impoundments are being devoured these days by an explosion of people fishing for trout, without any background or understanding of either the character of the trout or the centuries of tradition surrounding the sport. Past experience with bass or walleyes or bluefish has not prepared them for the skittish behavior of a trout on hard-fished waters, and their experiences in fishing for other species provide no prologue to the poetry and ethic of trout fishing or its centuries of contemplative literature.

And these hordes will have no one to teach them its gentle truths in future years, no father or grandfather or uncle in baggy tweeds and worn sweater, with a closetful of exquisite split-cane rods and a library of well-thumbed fishing books. The world of primeval trees and crystalline little streams is dwindling, and our aspiring trout fishermen are condemned to finding riffles filled with bedsprings, beer cans, tires, milk bottles, golf clubs, bumper jacks, and other refuse. It is an unthinkable sickness of the mind that can push rusting farm machinery into a crystalline riffle, or jettison a half-dozen rotting truck tires into a beautiful pool.

Memories are as important as the fishing itself, and their enjoyment depends greatly on solitude and the consideration of others along the stream.

Walton observed more than three centuries ago that angling was a contemplative sport, best attuned to the poetic moods and pastoral rhythms of life. His classic *Compleat Angler* added that a man who would become a skillful angler must combine the qualities of searching intelligence and powers of observation, but also a good measure of curiosity and optimism and patience. It might be argued that patience itself is the single most important quality in the character of a fly fisherman. It is equally true in our time of hard-fished waters and the cacophony of urban life. Our ethics and manners and philosophy play an increasingly critical role in the modern practice of our sport, and to Walton's historic prescription of hope and patience we must add the spice called charity.

Rhea Topping

Man's Best Friend: Should You Take Your Dog Fishing?

*T*alk about a can of worms! This subject is so controversial that I almost lost a good friend over our differences of opinion. And, folks, that's exactly what it boils down to. There is no right or wrong, no rule which dictates that one must *never* take one's canine pal along on a fly fishing excursion.

Lee Wulff used to say, "Time is something you can never give back." A dear friend told me that once. So, regardless of the application, keep that phrase in mind and decide whether taking Fido along could possibly be detrimental to anyone else's fishing time.

I am what people call a "dog person." In fact, I don't think I have ever met a bad person who loved dogs. I mention this to qualify the fact that I still feel that dogs don't really belong in most fly fishing scenarios. At least, not when there's even the most remote chance that you might meet another angler and jeopardize their fishing.

I have had two days of fishing ruined by someone else's dogs.

Disaster #1

It was the first afternoon of my first experience fishing for Atlantic salmon. We were on the Miramichi in Eastern Canada, and the fishing had not been spectacular for some time, attributed largely to netting and poaching problems on the river. As it was fairly late, we went to the Home Pool, which was close by, and which had consistently had the best numbers of fish recently. We were a group of eight, mostly strangers, and we used the traditional rotation system. Suddenly, this lovely lab jumped off the bank into the river, and proceeded to paddle between me and the angler just upstream who, in fact, was the dog's owner. The two of them thought this was great fun. A nice refreshing swim across to the far bank and back, and several "good girls" later, I thought my guide was going to have a stroke. He was apoplectic. He grumbled, "Might as well call it a day . . . that dog will have put every fish down in Home Pool. There's NO chance of anyone hooking a salmon tonight!" And he was right.

To this day, the owners aren't aware that their dog had the slightest influence on the fishing that afternoon. Nor do they realize that they may potentially have ruined the already-difficult-enough chance of landing an Atlantic salmon that afternoon for several other anglers. Who really knows? Perhaps we would not have had any hook-ups that afternoon anyway. But here is an incident, stemming from ignorance, not malice— an incident that could have, and should have, been avoided.

Disaster #2

The Beaverhead was high, and the recent rain had affected the visibility. Nevertheless, it was a beautiful, sunny fall afternoon in Twin Bridges, Montana. My friend, Annette, had invited us over from Livingston to fish with her. We loaded our gear into her husband's drift boat and trailered it to the put-in just outside of town. As we were backing it into the river, a large black lab, sans collar, came dripping and shaking out of the river onto the loading ramp, with a large tree limb in his mouth. We tried to ignore him, but that was not what he had in mind at all. As we set off down the swollen Beaverhead towards the Big Hole, our new best friend swam alongside, limb in tow. Whatever bank we would maneuver over to, to fish the pockets, Mr. Lab would get there first. We traversed that river a hundred times, and each time, there he was. What a lovely dog, a great swimmer, with tremendous retrieving instincts.

By then, I was enjoying him far more than either my fanatical fishing friend, Carole, or Annette, the self-appointed rower of the day. I thought she was going to bean him with the oar on more than one occasion. Five hours of floating with that lab, and not a single fish—natch. I finally convinced them to let me put him in the boat, as he was not only really tired, but we had traveled so far from the put-in that there was no way the poor dog could have found his way home—particularly across cattle country, where gun-bearing ranchers are prone to be rather protective of their stock.

I took a series of photos of this retrieving fool during the course of the float trip, and I use them as a very effective example in the Dog vs. Dog Controversy section of my slide show on Fly Fishing Etiquette—it gets the point across.

Of course there are exceptions to every rule, and many, many anglers get great pleasure out of taking their dogs along on fishing trips, and many are perfectly behaved and cause no problems. It is not for me to judge, or even suggest any rule against doing this. But, for those who do, please remember: It's fine as long as it doesn't affect other anglers.

Ed reconsiders the value of a stealthy approach to a trout stream while fishing with a retriever.

And on the other side of the coin, here's a story about a great fishing dog.

RHEA TOPPING

Chester LaFontaine: A Catch and Release Canine

Chester fished with Gary for nearly ten seasons and appeared in the fly fishing videos *Successful Fly Fishing Strategies*.

Gary swore that Chester was "the Einstein of dogs"; that he was fully bilingual in canine and English, and that he could take Chester absolutely anywhere, including the Little Lehigh in Pennsylvania, and that the dog would be perfectly behaved and not disturb man nor fish. That's quite a reputation to live up to! This is how Gary related the story to me.

On this particular day, Gary and Chester were fishing with a friend on one of the many prolific rivers near Deer Lodge, Montana. The friend was some distance downstream of them, and hooked a fairly sizable whitefish. Now, some people feel very strongly that whitefish are a nuisance, a junk fish, and can ruin a good day of trout fishing. The best solution is to eliminate the species. Obviously this guy was of that school, and so, without giving it any thought, the fellow removed the hook and tossed the unfortunate fish up on the bank. It landed about 30 feet from the river's edge in the tall grass.

Chester, being the perfect dog and never missing a trick, had keenly observed the hook-up, the hook removal, *and* the whitefish-from-the-river-removal. He had never seen any fish harmed in all his angling years. Furthermore, he could see no reason to distinguish a whitefish from any other species. A fish was a fish was a fish.

Out of the water (where he had been helping Gary locate trout), up the bank, Chester to the rescue. He put his nose to the poor fish's side and proceeded to nudge it, inch by inch, slowly down the hill in the direction of the water, from whence it came. This was no easy feat—we're talking tough conditions, folks—bumpy terrain, high grass, stones, and quite a distance. Had Chester learned this technique at a previous Easter Egg Rolling Party, perhaps?

Slowly, carefully, the old dog literally worked the whitefish back down the embankment and into the water. Unfortunately, the fish immediately turned belly up. Again, this was something Chester had never witnessed. He was used to seeing fish released right side up, and then swim quickly away. He knew there was something terribly wrong. He knew fish weren't supposed to swim off upside down, so being "the perfect angling dog," Chester took his paw and, ever so gently, rolled it over in the water, right side up. Within a few seconds, the fish took one last look at Chester, and beat it downstream as fast as it could swim.

This is a true story—no exaggeration—there were witnesses, and I saw the slide sequence of this event with my own disbelieving eyes.

Gary LaFontaine and Chester

GARY LAFONTAINE

1947–2002

Gary LaFontaine began writing about fly fishing when he was fifteen years old. Author, lecturer, publisher, father, psychologist, scientist, and perpetual student of the art and beauty of fly fishing, his best-selling books include *Caddisflies, The Dry Fly,* and *Trout Flies—Proven Patterns.*

LaFontaine represented the other side of the coin with respect to fishing with canine companions. Anyone who fished with him before his death in 2002 knows that he was never without his faithful angling cohort, Chester, who was the epitome of the perfectly trained fishing dog. To quote Gary, "He would never bother anyone else and that's good etiquette."

However, Gary was quick to agree that one should never take an untrained dog fishing, if there is even the most remote possibility of disturbing someone else's day. Therefore, he agreed to also share a tale of his daughter's dog, Enuk, whose fishing etiquette is not as perfect.

Enuk

Fishing Among the Barbarians
The Book Mailer, 1997

*E*ven walking around Deer Lodge with my daughter's dog, Enuk, is quite an experience. Brave men cross the street;

women grab their babies and run screaming for the nearest storefront doorway.

Taking him fishing is a guaranteed disaster, but I truly love him (everyone knows I'm goofy about dogs) and there was at least one benefit to having him with me last summer.

He's purebred Malamute: longhaired, very large, and very beautiful. I'm the only one he'll listen to and that is conditional (he sets the conditions). His name means "pretty wolf" in Eskimo.

I went to the Missouri River and it was so crowded that I couldn't even find a place to fish. I kept checking my secret haunts, and finally found a channel against a backwater island.

Enuk crossed the channel and ran over the top of the island and disappeared. Usually he runs in the water whenever I'm going to cast and looks for trout. This time I had a pod of sipping rainbows all to myself.

Before I could make my first cast, a drift boat pulled into the upper end of the channel, no more than 50 feet away from me. The guide climbed out and gave me a long dirty look that said, "We're here and there's nothing you can do about it."

His clients looked like son and father. They sounded like foreigners (anyone east of Billings) to me. And they couldn't even look me in the eye. They just waded in and started fishing right above me.

In a few minutes the old man, a little guy about five foot and a hop, hooked a nice jumping rainbow. At that moment Enuk came bounding over the hill. The same Enuk—but by now he had swum in the river, rolled in the mud, and run through brambles.

He came off that crest full speed and hit that little old man right behind the knees. He wanted that fish, but the guy was flat in the water and Enuk's favorite game with my dog is to get on top of him and push him under the surface. He was just so happy at finding someone who wanted to play "Drown the Mutt" with him! The old man would try to get up, screaming and sputtering, and Enuk would knock him back down.

The younger fellow came running up and reached out for the animal. Enuk spun around, so happy he was grinning (which shows a lot of teeth) because his second favorite game is "Grab the Arm."

The young guy starts backing away, wailing, "Is that a wolf? Is that a wolf?" I'm downstream wailing, "My God, it's a wolf! My God, it's a wolf!"

Enuk turned back to the old guy, who had climbed halfway up, and hit him with a clean shot right between the shoulder blades, driving him out into the river and completely under water.

The guide came running down, took one look at Enuk and decided not to annoy him. He turned to me, huffed downstream, and asked loudly, "Is that your dog?"

"Yes, it is. I keep him around to keep jerks like you out of my water. Why?" He could argue with me (while his client was drowning) or be nice. He changed to nice. "Look, I'm sorry. The river is so crowded and I had to find a spot for them to fish. Could you please get your dog?"

I grabbed Enuk and they got the old man, crying, hyperventilating, and hysterical, into the boat. They never even said thanks. They never even waved goodbye.

(Gary wrote, "This story was certainly embellished, for the fun of publishing it in my newsletter, *The Book Mailer*. The 'victim' wrote a great letter, which appeared in the next issue of my newsletter. He said I took him and his son fishing the next two days, which was, in fact, true.")

The legend of the Ghost Wolf spread quickly. For the rest of the season I could show up anywhere on the river and within minutes I'd have a half mile of water in either direction all to myself. Who says that there's no on-stream etiquette among the barbarians anymore? There's always some way to skin a cat, but this one is on the far side of the manners spectrum of fly fishing with man's best friend.

STAN BRADSHAW
Helena, Montana

Bradshaw is the principal in Greycliff Publishing with his wife, Glenda. He works for Trout Unlimited as counsel for the Montana Water Project. Prior to that he was the Resource Director for Montana Trout Unlimited. He also served on the State Water Plan Advisory Council. From 1976 to 1979, he worked for the Montana Department of Health and Environmental Sciences on subdivision and water quality issues. From 1981 through 1986, he worked for the Montana Department of Fish, Wildlife and Parks, where he was chief counsel.

He's an accomplished white-water canoeist, enthusiastic fly fisherman, and avid skier.

River Etiquette in Dry Times

From *River Safety: A Floater's Guide,*
Greycliff Publishing Co., 2000

If there is one rule as immutable as death and taxes, it's that a drought is wickedly democratic—ranchers and farmers, gardeners, outfitters and guides, anglers and other recreational floaters . . . everybody takes a hit. When you put two drought years back to back, the damage is all the more severe. As a drought progresses, rivers decline, forests burn, fish die, and tempers fray. Human nature being what it is, anglers being anglers, and floaters being floaters, we'll likely be on the rivers while we can. But even before they get hot and go dry, they'll likely be low. And low water can accelerate conflict among river users and exacerbate damage to the river. So here are a few rules that, if followed, should reduce the decibel level and soften our impact on a resource we all treasure.

1. Remember, you're not the only person on the river, and it's not your private playpen. Don't crowd other boats or anglers. This should be a cardinal rule, and violation of it should result in swift and brutal punishment—a lifetime sentence to porta-potty duty or 24 hours straight of irritating music to be chosen by the victim of your crowding—something along those lines, anyway.

2. If you're in a boat and you see an angler wading, give her some space. This requires looking ahead to anticipate the angler. If there isn't space to give, try to go behind her so you don't screw up the fishing. And if you can't pass without going over the water she's fishing (a pretty common problem on rivers like the Smith), apologize and

try to get through as quickly as you can. A well-placed apology can go a long way toward soothing hard feelings.

3. Don't hog the launch area. There's nothing more irritating than having to sit and cool your heels while the people ahead of you unpack their gear, inflate their boats, repack their food, discuss world events, and generally hold things up right in the middle of the boat ramp. So don't do it to others. Unload your stuff away from the launch area so others can get on the river while you're getting ready.

4. If you get to the put-in and it's full-to-overflowing, go somewhere else. Some put-ins, especially on places like the Blackfoot River, have specific vehicle limits. On the Blackfoot, those put-ins have often been donated by adjoining landowners. Respect the vehicle limits.

5. If you bring your dog along, keep it under control. If you can't control it, don't bring it. It's not amusing to have a strange dog come lumbering into your lunch spot, snuffling in your food packs and pooping in the picnic area. So don't inflict your dog on others.

6. Try to keep the decibel level down to something less than a dull roar. Most floaters aren't there just for the unbridled pleasure of listening to your favorite boom-box tunes or to hear your group discussion from hundreds of yards away. And if your tunes are so precious to you that you can't go on the river without them, stay home.

7. Respect the rights of adjoining landowners. In Montana, while we enjoy what amounts to a public easement to float through private lands, that right usually ends above the ordinary high-water mark. This should be a no-brainer.

8. Avoid behavior that damages the natural resources on the river. Don't litter. Don't drag your anchor (if you have one)

along the bottom of the river. And don't take your axe to the trees or decide to cut a custom log table, or otherwise trash the streamside vegetation. Leave any rocks or historic artifacts where you find them. Respect any wildlife you encounter. Don't harass animals and don't feed them. If you see animals nesting or mating, don't go up and butt in on them. Leave them alone.

9. If you're playing at a rapid or at some other spot on the river, pay attention to boats coming through the rapid and yield to the through traffic. This goes back to Rule 1.

10. Know the regulations and obey them. If a river has special regulations, obey them. They will usually address some problem specific to the river. Don't become part of the problem by flouting the regulations.

11. If you're camping, try to use established campsites, and, in any event, practice no-trace camping. Don't alter a spot to create a campsite. Focus your activities in areas of minimal vegetation. Even in a wet year, don't build a fire unless you really need one. This year, don't build one, *period.* And if the urge to gaze deeply into the bowels of a fire seems overwhelming, just keep reminding yourself about last year's wildfires.

12. Dispose of wastes properly. Use public toilets where they exist. When you can't use a public toilet (and sometimes you just can't wait) pack out any solid wastes or dig a cat hole 6 to 8 inches deep at least 200 feet from the water. If you're floating through private lands, the 200-foot option may not be available, and you may just have to hold it or pack it out. If you do a cat hole, cover and disguise it when you're done. In areas of heavy use, the cat hole option is simply not good enough. That's where a good porta-potty

comes in. Pack out anything you have packed in. If you wash dishes, carry water 200 feet away from streams or lakes and use small amounts of biodegradable soap. Scatter strained dishwater.

Finally, at some point this summer the water on many, if not most, of our trout streams is going to get dangerously warm for the fish. At around 70 degrees F., trout are barely hanging on. You don't have to wait for a state-ordained closure—just quit fishing those heat-stressed waters. Exercise a little self-restraint. This goes back to Rule 8, respecting wildlife.

In the meantime, if you catch a fish and intend to release it, land it as quickly as you can and release it with a minimum of handling. This would be a good summer to just skip the trophy photos, unless you can take them while keeping the fish in the water. A fish that bounces around the bottom of your boat while you scramble to strike the trophy pose is likely a dead fish.

That's about it. If we all exercise a little respect and courtesy while we're on the water, it will make it easier for us to get through what promises to be a long, hot summer.

Part Three

OCEANS, FLATS, AND SALT WATER

In salt water, the odds are stacked against the fly caster. It's a harsh environment, unforgiving of angler error or oversight. You may only get one shot a day, after what may be hours of preparation and waiting.

Saltwater fly fishing is about eliminating variables—and the angler often has more than he can handle of his own. Introduce outside interference and bad manners and the proposition becomes more than frustrating. It becomes futile. The salt, especially the flats, has spawned its own set of manners, and they are critical lessons that must be learned if you choose to venture into this demanding and rewarding angling arena.

©Anthony Traver

Retaliation.

National Marine Fisheries Service

The National Marine Fisheries Service has adopted a code that promotes ethical fishing behavior by anglers. The American Sportfishing Association, the Coastal Conservation Association, the Recreational Fishing Alliance, and Trout Unlimited all contributed to the development of this code.

> "The code gives us an official avenue to foster sound resource management attitudes and actions with our angling constituents. It is a strong step by the agency to meet its commitment to work with our recreational fisheries constituents as partners in ensuring a healthy marine environment."
>
> —Rolland Schmitten, Director of the
> National Marine Fisheries Service

> "While the code may seem self-evident to some, it was developed with a broad base of angler support, and the final result outlines simple actions that, if practiced by all, will benefit the quality of the angling experience today and for future generations."
>
> —Dick Schaefer, Chief of the Intergovernmental and
> Recreational Fisheries Office for the Fisheries Service

The Fisheries Service will provide the code to anglers, fishing clubs, bait and tackle shops, and fishing boat operators through a variety of cards, stickers, and posters.

The Code of Angling Ethics:

· Promotes, through education and practice, ethical behavior in the use of aquatic resources.

· Values and respects the aquatic environment and all living things in it.

· Avoids spilling and never dumps any pollutants, such as gasoline and oil, into the aquatic environment.

· Disposes of all trash, including worn lines, leaders, and hooks, in appropriate containers, and helps to keep fishing sites litter-free.

· Takes all precautionary measures necessary to prevent the spread of exotic plants and animals, including live baitfish, into non-native habitats.

· Learns and obeys angling and boating regulations, and treats other anglers, boaters, and property owners with courtesy and respect.

· Respects property rights, and never trespasses on private lands or waters.

· Keeps no more fish than needed for consumption, and never wastefully discards fish that are retained.

· Practices conservation by carefully handling and releasing alive all fish that are unwanted or prohibited by regulation, as well as other animals that may become hooked or entangled accidentally.

· Uses tackle and techniques that minimize harm to fish when engaging in "catch and release" angling.

Vlad Evanoff

Evanoff often said, "Nobody ever becomes perfect at fishing; there is always something new to learn." In addition to doing his own illustrations, the Brooklyn, New York, native made a living writing about fishing. He covered everything from tackle to fresh- and saltwater fish, to lures and bait and sportsmanship. He authored *A Complete Guide to Fishing, Surf Fishing Tips, The Art of Bottom Fishing, How to Make Fishing Lures, Modern Fishing Tackle,* and *Natural Baits for Fishermen,* and edited *Fishing Secrets of the Experts.*

Problems

From *Surf Fishing,* A. S. Barnes & Co.,
The Barnes Sport Library, 1948

Almost every book written about hunting and fishing touches on conservation and sportsmanship. More and more people are turning to the outdoors for relaxation and recreation. The increase in the number of anglers and hunters in recent years has multiplied and the toll of game has been enormous. Further to aggravate the situation many of the newcomers are unfamiliar with the laws, while others do not care to observe them. What can we do to improve this unhealthy situation?

Probably in no other type of fishing are there so many secretive and close-mouthed anglers as in surfcasting. Many experienced surf anglers refuse to reveal any information to the novice. And yet, the average surf caster is more than willing to play the game and help a fellow fisherman.

However, our greatest evil is the pollution of waters and depletion of spawning grounds. To make things worse, dams are built in rivers and swamps and marshes are drained or filled in. It is my belief that the number of surf anglers can be doubled or even tripled and still enjoy the sport of good fishing if we clean up our rivers and prevent any further drainage or filling in of inland waters.

There's no doubt that the increase of surf anglers has created a problem in the crowding of some of our most popular fishing spots. This calls for fine sportsmanship among our surf anglers. Every one of us should live up to the unwritten laws of the sport.

One of these is that the man who arrives first on the scene is entitled to his spot. Too many anglers disregard this rule until casting becomes difficult and dangerous. Some even go so far as to steal another's spot when he leaves it for a moment to change baits.

Another surf caster who lacks sportsmanship is the fellow who casts in any direction he pleases. He never hesitates to cast over your line. This is the same man who usually refuses to reel in his line when another angler has hooked a fish near him.

Still another bad habit is the taking of undersized fish. Most of the offenders are enthusiastic beginners who have just caught their first striper.

There are others who consider their trip a failure if they don't catch the right species or one of a certain size. These men are going after "record fish." The spirit of competition is a fine thing but it can be overdone when it comes to fishing.

Any man who has been fishing for any length of time finds out that the fish itself is the smallest part of the game. There's no sport like fishing for making friends. The pleasure gained in meeting new friends and watching them grow into old friends over the years is really gratifying. You will find a comradeship that is rarely present in other sports.

On the positive side, I've seen many an angler share his flies with a less fortunate stranger. And many a trip has been saved from failure by a surf angler who gave some badly needed tackle to another man. These men are in a class very few anglers attain, but it is a goal all of us should work toward, for only then can we truly say that we fish for sport.

FLIP PALLOT
Mims, Florida

Flip Pallot's name is synonymous with saltwater fly fishing and the Florida Keys. Outdoor writer, freelance photographer, guide, U.S. Coast Guard–licensed captain, avid duck hunter, and a consultant for numerous sportfishing companies are only a few of the occupations that fill Pallot's busy schedule.

He has produced a number of fishing videos and television series, not the least of which is the popular *Walkers Cay Chronicles*. He supports the Sierra Club, Ducks Unlimited, the Izaak Walton League, the N.R.A., and the Nature Conservancy, and is on the Board of Advisors of the Everglades Protection Association.

A Story of Bonefishing Etiquette

*S*ome many years ago I was bonefishing with a friend on the ocean-side flats of Key Largo. The tide was low and rising. It was April, in the late afternoon, and we were enjoying the presence of lots of bonefish and very little other traffic. All at once we heard a skiff in the distance and spotted it heading toward us from the north. We also noticed that it was running right along the edge of the flat and must certainly have been frightening every bonefish in its path. The skiff finally got within 100 yards of us and shut down. The occupants hauled out fly rods and a push pole and began poling along the flat in the very same direction that we were poling. The flat was perhaps ten miles long following the shoreline of the island. We were now rudely cut off by a skiff having run the entire shoreline. To make matters worse, these guys were now poling along right in front of us.

By way of an excuse for my behavior, I must submit I was much younger then and perhaps less wise. In any case, I put up my poling pole, fired up the engine, and ran a very close circle around the intruders, and if memory serves, uttered an oath as I completed the circle.

Now, years later, I am quite ashamed of my actions on that occasion. I realize that those folks had no idea what they had done wrong. They had no notion that they had inadvertently committed a breach of etiquette, and I missed an opportunity to explain it to them. Moreover, I was ruder than they, especially since I knew the neighborhood and they obviously did not.

I've long since forgiven them, but not myself. Time or experience has taught me that there will from now on be more and more newcomers to fly fishing. They will need to learn etiquette along with fishing skills, and it will be the responsibility of the rest of us to help them learn.

The truth is that we need them. Yes, there will be crowds and often we will see others in our favorite, secret spot, but without them we have no voice. Without them there will be nets, commercial fishing atrocities, habitat destruction, loss of resources, and worst of all, loss of liberty.

I wish I knew to whom to apologize for my actions on that long ago bonefish flat. Maybe one day I'll get the chance.

CAPTAIN FRED CHRISTIAN
Salem, Massachusetts

Fred Christian has been fishing the waters of Boston's North Shore for thirty years, and has fished from Maine to Florida, the Bahamas, and Grand Cayman Island. He has served as national director and treasurer of the Northeastern Council of the Federation of Flyfishers, and director for the Coastal Conservation Association of New England and Massachusetts (CCAMA). He is currently a member of the Recreational Advisory Panel to the New England Marine Fisheries. A fly-fishing guide and charter captain, FFF-certified casting instructor, and boat-handling instructor, he works at the Boston Fly Fishing Company out of Boston and Marblehead, Massachusetts.

Some Thoughts on Saltwater Etiquette

Saltwater anglers need to practice good etiquette, just like everyone else. The overwhelming vastness of the ocean should not make a difference in angling manners. One occasionally sees a callousness towards both the handling of the fish and towards fellow anglers. The depth and breadth of the sea appear to make breaches of etiquette appear to go unnoticed. For instance, with no one close enough to observe your activities it's easier to discard line or leader materials in the water than dealing with them in a responsible fashion. If the water were a small pristine trout stream this would be less likely to happen.

When the sea is alive with fish, it seems that it can't possibly make a difference of how many fish we kill. But in fact it does, because this type of attitude and behavior is catching, and the numbers killed are accumulative. Often I hear, "Why should I be responsible when others are not?" Many species have been abused to the point of extinction by such attitudes.

Believe it or not, crowding on the ocean is a constant issue. I believe there are two major factors involved. One is the psychology of the mob, where everyone wants to be doing what the other angler is doing (usually the first one there). There are days when I am the first and only angler for as far as I can see. Then, the next boat heading out will invariably head in my direction and start fishing within close proximity of my boat. Usually this causes a chain reaction, and eventually there are a considerable number of boats clustered together. Twenty to eighty feet is way too close, whereas a quiet, well-planned approach to within 100 feet or more could be acceptable.

I suppose when they see that I am catching fish, they figure that even with all the thousands of fishing spots, my spot is where *all* the fish are.

The second factor is insecurity. The angler either believes that a particular spot is the only place he can catch fish, or he or she has no confidence in their ability to locate fish. This type of angler will bully their way into "their" spot, crowding other anglers and creating a commotion, which scares the fish and often ruins the spot for everyone.

In summation, I find that we saltwater fishers have many more opportunities than freshwater anglers to exercise good etiquette. The mere fact that saltwater species travel and range further in continually changing waters than most freshwater species provides more flexibility and more reasons to "get away from the pack."

Billy Pate
Islamorada, Florida

Pate has held more significant IGFA world records than any other angler, including a 188-pound tarpon record that has stood since 1983. He was the first to land blue and black marlin on fly, and the first to catch all six bill-fish species on fly. His Islamorada tackle shop/travel agency, World Wide Sportsman, put many of the world's finest fishing spots within reach of American anglers.

Courtesy on the Flats (Its Importance for Tomorrow)

In the mid-60s, I began to explore the Florida Keys back-country around Islamorada in my own flats boat. There were few private boats there in those days and only about thirty flats guides there. Everyone knew each other and there was outstanding courtesy amongst everyone.

Courtesy is not the first thing one thinks about when they begin to explore a new area and way of fishing. One thinks of navigation and maps, one thinks of boating techniques, and fishing equipment and strategies, and the tides and the winds and the sun and water. We have to learn the habits of the fish and the seasons and what attracts them.

Several of the guides of those days were generous in helping me learn many of the details, especially my long-time friend and business partner, George Hommell, who at the time was my fishing guide. Thank goodness these men explained to me the extreme importance of courtesy to other boats, and the many unwritten rules everyone practiced when other boats were near, especially when approaching a boat that had reached a spot before you arrived there. In addition to being courteous because they were your friends, the unwritten rules enabled techniques that helped everyone to catch more fish.

Courtesy involved many aspects. It was necessary to learn from which direction to approach an area, whether or not another boat was already there. Did you approach another boat from the east or west or south or north? Upwind or downwind? Up sun or down sun? How close to come with the big engine, and how close to pick up the poling pole? And now, how close to pole to the next boat? What to do if you hooked up a fish, or if the other boat hooked up? Pole or fire up? Where were the fish lying? Or if they were traveling, what was their track? How to know the track and how not to motor over it, when coming or going?

These were just some of the courtesy considerations necessary for 50 or 100 great fishing spots in the area. But as time went on another important aspect of courtesy became very large in my mind and the minds of other regulars on the Islamorada flats. This had to do with the tracks of the tarpon and bonefish, daily and seasonally, along certain pathways and inside of various salt water "lakes" and "bights" bounded by the shallow banks of the keys.

As more flats-type boats became available the last three decades of the century, there were many new faces driving many boats we didn't recognize. Unfortunately many of the newcomers did not take the time to learn the courtesies the old timers practiced, and perhaps some just didn't care. The result was boats running over the tracks of the tarpon, for instance, as they moved from Cape Sable on the southern tip of Florida through the flats of the Keys for 25 miles or so to the bridges of the Keys bordering the Atlantic Ocean. Another track was outside the Keys on the Ocean side from Key Largo to Key West. And the boats would also run through many of the shallow five-foot-deep lakes where the fish would be laying up or feeding or milling slowly around. These actions, in addition to scaring the fish for nearby anglers, drove the fish deep beneath the surface and farther out to sea, away from the shallow banks.

I believe that the population of tarpon and bonefish is as plentiful today as ever, but we don't see as many. They are deep and wide. And unfortunately they are also spookier, and more difficult to tease with a fly.

The same principles hold true for Homosassa and Boca Grande on Florida's west coast. At these two great tarpon fishing areas, as in the Keys, there are more joyriders, week-enders, jet skis, and big boats cruising around, not fishing. They don't intend to spook your fish but they often do. I have encouraged the outdoor writers of newspapers in these areas to seek the cooperation of folks who are out enjoying the weekend, but not necessarily fishing.

In 1974 a few of us from the Keys went up to Homosassa to

give the giant tarpon that we had heard about a try. It was fabulous and more Keys guides and their anglers came in succeeding years. Fortunately their tradition of courtesy became respected in the Homosassa area, even though the tranquility can be spoiled occasionally by a boat, which unknowingly strays into the tarpon fishing area.

All of us who try to practice courtesy with our fellow fisherman must try also to respond in a courteous way to those who unintentionally intrude on our sacred fishing grounds. It takes some lip biting, especially with jet skis, and some time lost from fishing to try to explain in a friendly manner that we are trying to catch some very spooky fish that are easily scared by the sound of a roaring engine. But if we all spread the word in a friendly and courteous way, our fishing chances may no longer diminish, and in fact, could start to return to the good old days. On the flats our future fun depends so much on courtesy from all sides.

Tom Jindra
New Orleans, Louisiana

A journalist of twenty-nine years, Jindra currently chairs the Casting Instructor Certification Program's Board of Governors for the Federation of Fly Fishers (FFF) and was also the former National President of FFF. He has fished for numerous species throughout North America and the world. His expertise is saltwater flats.

Rethinking Conservation and the Ocean
Fly Fish America, 1998

I was listening to a report on the deteriorating state of the world's fisheries when a particular sentence jumped out to grab my attention: Scientists and managers are rethinking the concept of the sea as an unlimited resource. Rethinking?

I can only hope the reporter misstated the issue. That the people with whom we entrust our resources are too experienced to believe in unlimited resources and that any rethinking occurred long before now. Our history is simply filled with too many examples of species obliterated through mankind's abuse to accept such fantasy.

But I'm left with the uncomfortable feeling that there are those in the scientific community and among our fisheries managers who still believe in oceans so vast that they can never be overfished.

After all, it wasn't so long ago that the experts allowed the destruction of king mackerel stocks in the Gulf of Mexico in belief that the fishery was self-regulating. This meant that commercial fishing would stop on its own when the schools became too thin for netting to be economically viable. And once the netting stopped, the fishery would replenish itself. Or such was the theory. A decade after an outcry from sportsmen halted the destruction, the kings have begun to return in the Gulf. But even now, the fishery is only a shadow of its former self.

Were lessons learned? Perhaps. But then, I'm left wondering why the National Oceanic and Atmospheric Administration would now offer satellite tracking of fish schools to anyone who wants it. When we already have the ability to track down and wipe out a species, is it really wise to add even more firepower to the arsenal? Isn't that the same kind of thinking that left our New England and salmon fisheries in such a shambles?

I confess that my feelings about such management theories go even deeper, that in my love for the coast I find I resent those who would turn our marine environments into nothing more than a vast food factory. Just as I resent those who would turn all our inland streams into a maze of concrete and culverts.

I love the sea because it is both beautiful and wild, and I have no qualms in sharing it with others, commercial or otherwise, who respect that beauty and wildness. But we must all get beyond the notion that the sea is something we can manage or control to our own ends. Rather, it is something for which we must care.

As a first step, we must recognize that we can't truly care for the sea while continuing unfettered abuse. Therefore, it is time we allowed the myth of the unlimited resource to die.

Author Unknown

Protecting Fish Habitat: A Guide for Fishermen and Boaters

The Coast

Anyone who's spent time on the water can appreciate the beauty, power, and richness of our bays and oceans. Whether fishing for sport or work, fishermen are especially in tune with the benefits of clean and bountiful marine waters.

More and more people are being drawn to the water. By the year 2010, more than 53 percent of the people in the U.S. are expected to live within 50 miles of the coast. With the increasing population, there will be an increase in threats to the richness and beauty of the waters which provided the attraction in the first place. Even boating related activities can contribute substantially to the degradation or loss of important coastal resources.

Important Fish Habitat
Estuaries and near-shore waters are vital rearing grounds for the vulnerable young of many important fish and shellfish species. Unfortunately, these areas are also the ones that are most frequently exposed to pollution from vessel activity. Even when greatly diluted, pollutants can have harmful impacts.

How Small Impacts Add Up
One quart of engine oil spilled in one million quarts of sea-water will kill half of the exposed crab larvae. Negative impacts

are aggravated when detergents or soaps are use to "treat" these spills. These pollutants reduce the amount of oxygen in the water, impair the functioning of fish gills, and reduce the ability of seabirds to stay warm and dry.

When untreated sewage is discharged rather than disposed of at a pump-out station, it can result in bacterial contamination as much as 10,000 times greater than that of treated sewage, which severely impacts the harvest ability of shellfish such as clams and oysters.

When vessels are being fueled or topped off, up to 8 ounces of fuel can spurt out and spill into the water. Although some of the chemicals in gas and diesel fuel evaporate rapidly, many toxic compounds remain behind in the water column. Multiplying these relatively small spills by the number of boats in a busy marina and the number of boating days per year can add up to big water quality problems.

Other activities associated with fishing or boating that can cause serious problems include sanding toxic hull paint over the water, littering, and spilling or washing cleaners, paints or solvents into drains or directly into the water. Boat propellers and wakes can disturb submerged aquatic vegetation and can cause bank erosion.

What We Can Do
It is important for us to realize the impact of our combined actions, and minimize them. Read on to learn some of the things we can do to help protect fish habitat.

Underway
  · Keep trash from blowing overboard; bring it back to
    port for proper disposal.

· Avoid boating in shallow waters, especially those with submerged vegetation.

· Follow "no wake" postings, and keep wakes down in shallow or near shore areas to prevent erosion.

· Never discharge treated or untreated sewage; wait to use pump-out facilities.

· Report oil spills or debris violations to the proper authorities.

At the Dock

· Recycle used oil and filters, batteries and antifreeze.

· Use shore side restrooms and pump out facilities.

· Tell your friends and fellow fishermen about the importance of protecting fish habitat.

· Minimize fish waste disposal in marina waters.

· Encourage your marina to provide facilities for recycling and dry dock repair.

· Whenever possible, do repairs and painting in dry dock; keep paints and paint chips away from the water.

On Your Boat

· Use oil absorbent materials in your bilge and for spill cleanup.

· Refrain from using detergents and bilge cleaners; never pump them overboard.

· Use the smallest amount of the least toxic products available when cleaning.

· Be careful when fueling; catch any overflow with petroleum absorbent materials.

· Install an overflow alarm on your fuel tank.

· When doing small repairs, sanding or scraping, use tarps to catch pollutants.
· Avoid boating in shallow waters, especially those with submerged vegetation.
· Keep wakes down in shallow or near shore areas to prevent erosion.

Each person's small efforts add up to a big difference for fish habitat.

Tell your friends and fellow fishermen about the importance of fish habitat and the simple things they can do every day to protect it.

Part Four

OF BOATS AND GUIDES

Myriad kinds of fishing get done with guides in and out of boats, and while both guides and boats can add immeasurably to the angling experience, each has its own rules of etiquette. The accomplished, polite angler needs to be expert in the safe, courteous operation of a vehicle in the case of boats, and an expert in labor and business relations to enter into the guide/client relationship. These added dimensions create more opportunities for enjoyment, and more for oversight and conflict. But in the end, being a good boatman and a good client/fishing companion is a simple matter of common sense and remembering why you are on the water.

Author Unknown

The Angler-Guide Relationship

*F*ew human relationships are as fraught with problems as that of angler and angling guide. And the possibility of disappointment, frustration, and ill temper is as great as that for camaraderie, fellowship, and high-spirited good times.

When things go wrong on the water, each tends to blame the other, but the truth is seldom that simple.

Fly fisher and fly fishing guide are really responsible for the success of a fishing trip, and both must work at making the trip a success. The guide, because it's his job. The angler, because it's his time and money.

For both, happiness is at stake. Anyone can have a good fishing experience when the sky is blue, the wind is light, the water is right, and the fish are on the bite.

But darken the sky, crank up the wind, raise or lower the water, and put the fish in a sulk, and everyone's mettle and good will go on trial.

Bob Clouser
Middletown, Pennsylvania

The Clouser Deep Minnow is one of the most effective underwater fly patterns ever developed for both fresh and salt water—not a bad mark to have associated with your name, particularly if you make a living in the fly fishing industry.

Although a good portion of his time is spent guiding for smallmouth bass on the Susquehanna River, Bob stills finds time to teach fly fishing, casting, and tying, as well as lecture and write.

He has been recognized with the Warm Water Committee Achievement Award and the Dr. James Henshall Award presented by the Federation of Fly Fishers and the 1995 Conservation Award of the Year presented by the Susquehanna Smallmouth Alliance. He was also named Angler of the Year by *Fly Rod & Reel* magazine.

Boating Etiquette

1. Never cut off, or pull in front of, another boat that is approaching a fishing area.
2. Have respect for other boats that are anchored or drifting by not passing them at full speed.
3. It is polite to keep at least two casting lengths (a casting length should be at least 100 feet where I fish) between boats while fishing an area.
4. Don't cross the path of anglers while fishing from a drifting boat. If you must cross, allow at least three casting lengths in order not to spook their fish, or tangle in their lines. Do it at a no-wake or very slow speed.
5. If you are fishing from a boat and encounter wading fishermen, give them the right of way.
6. Never allow any trash or other unwanted items to be discarded overboard.
7. Passing a slow moving boat while it is approaching a dock or mooring area for the sole purpose of beating them to the dock is downright discourteous.
8. Before passing across a boat's wake, make sure you do not cross the fishing lines of a boat that is trolling lures.
9. When you prepare to launch a boat at a busy boat ramp, make sure that all preparation of gear and other necessary items is done before entering the launching area.
10. When you prepare to remove your boat from the water at a busy boat launching area, do it as quickly as possible. Load the boat on the trailer, drive it away from the launching area, and *then* do the necessary preparations needed for towing.

11. Never park any vehicle in or on any boat launching area, and that includes the turn-around sections.

12. Have patience with newcomers at boat launching ramps, offering your assistance in a friendly way.

13. Never throw any trash or other unwanted items onto the parking or launching areas of any boat launching facility.

14. Do not block any entrance or exit while preparing your boat for launching.

15. Never park your vehicle (boat and trailer) at any area, position, or space where it could interfere with another person's ingress or egress after launching your boat.

16. If you are loading your boat on a trailer at a busy boat ramp and it is after dark, make sure your headlights are turned off, and only your parking lights are turned on. This practice prevents the blinding of another boater that is backing his vehicle and trailer/boat down the launching ramp.

Row vs. Wade: the Great Western Fishing Controversy.

JOHN JURACEK
West Yellowstone, Montana

After a postcollege biology job with the Wyoming Fish and Game Department, John Juracek spent twenty years as a partner in Blue Ribbon Flies, West Yellowstone, Montana. He is the author of *Yellowstone: Photos of a Fly Fishing Landscape* and coauthor of *Fishing Yellowstone Hatches* and *Fly Patterns of Yellowstone*. He currently works part-time for Blue Ribbon during the fishing season, ties flies commercially during the winter, and fishes the waters around Yellowstone National Park.

On Hiring a Guide

I've watched people hire fishing guides here at Blue Ribbon for sixteen seasons now, and I hope I've seen all the reasons they do it. I've seen guides hired to be chauffeurs and babysitters, teachers and tour guides, manual laborers, oarsmen, counselors, comedians, drinking partners, companions—it's a long list. And, I've seen them hired so a client can catch fish.

I'm not here to condemn any reason anyone ever had, or, heaven forbid, will have, for wanting to hire a guide, except one. And that's to catch fish. That's right, hiring a guide so you can catch fish is a terrible idea. Why? Because catching fish on any given day is a crapshoot. It might happen and it might not. It's a waste of the guide's talents and abilities if that desire is all you bring to the table.

Why, then, should anyone hire a guide? While you may derive some benefit from any of the above mentioned reasons (depending on the guide, of course) I think it's safe to assume your money is best spent with one purpose in mind: learning how to catch fish. Not *catching* fish, mind you, but *learning how* to catch fish. There is a huge difference there.

Fish being what they are, well, sometimes they can be caught, sometimes not. It makes no difference who your guide is or what he does. But on any day you can learn to catch them, and that really is the crux of the issue. Teaching is what the guide is expert at—use him for that. Everything you take from a guide is yours forever, whether you use it tomorrow, the day after tomorrow, or ten years after. The point is that you always have it. This opportunity to acquire knowledge will always be, for me, the most legitimate reason for hiring a guide.

As I noted above though, it's not the only reason. After all, guides do make great companions, and it is a pleasure to spend a day with them. Many long friendships have started this way. Not only that, they are better oarsmen than most fishermen. So hire a guide for any number of reasons, whatever pleases you, but don't do it just to catch fish. While it may work out on any given day, I still feel that it shortchanges you and the guide. He has so much to teach, and we all have so much to learn.

STU APTE
Tavernier, Florida

Stu Apte was a Navy fighter pilot in the Korean War. He spent the next thirty-four years flying for Pan Am and pursuing his real passion, fly fishing, which he began in the mid-1940s.

He has held more than forty world records on fly and light tackle and has guided many anglers to records of their own.

The Stu Apte Tarpon Fly and Stu Apte Improved Blood Knot are standard items in saltwater fly fishing. The former has the distinction of adorning a United States postage stamp.

In 1971, Stu was inducted into the Fishing Hall of Fame. His book, *Stu Apte's Fishing in the Florida Keys,* has sold thousands of copies. He has appeared on numerous television shows and produced award-winning films and videos including *Tarpon Country* and *Quest for a Giant Tarpon.*

Etiquette for Guides and Clients
My Views on the Importance of Good Communication and Shared Responsibilities Between the Guide and the Client

*H*aving had the opportunity to be on both ends of a back-country skiff, as a guide for many years, and as an angler, I feel reasonably qualified to discuss what is proper etiquette from both a guide's and an angler's point of view.

From a guide's perspective

To begin with, a backcountry skiff is a rather small (16- to 18-foot) area that serves as a guide's office, sometimes for more than 30 days in a row. Most good guides like to work in a clean office, and will have their skiff spic-and-span each morning when greeting their clients for the day.

Here are a few suggestions that come to mind that all guides would hope their clients would be aware of:

The clients would be getting off on the right foot (so to speak) if they wear soft-soled boat shoes that will not leave black marks on the clean deck. It is also considerate to ask the guide where he/she would like you to put any trash or empty soft drink cans, as most guides have very specific places.

While on the fishing grounds, open and close any compartment lids as quietly as possible, and of course, try not to make any noise banging or kicking things in the boat. Guides take a lot of pride in producing fish for their anglers. There were quite a few times when I would shut off the engine more than a quarter of a mile away from the area I expected to fish, sometimes poling into the wind and into the current, in order to get the clients close to the still-undisturbed fish, only to have a second angler in the boat slam a compartment lid, spooking every fish in the entire area. Talk about having a small area get even smaller in a hurry!

The evening before your trip is the time to discuss the type of fishing and species of fish you would prefer to catch if the weather conditions, tides, and time of year permit. This is also a good time to discuss what type of tackle and how much tackle you should bring along. There is only a minimal amount of storage space in most backcountry skiffs. Most anglers were more than happy to use my equipment, knowing that it would be properly rigged for the type of fishing they would be doing.

The Florida Keys is the only area in the world that I know of where it is customary for the anglers to provide lunch for themselves and the guide. So, you might ask your guide if he has any preferences ahead of time. Back in the early 1960s I remember guiding for 100-plus days in a row. I can tell you that I got very tired of eating ham-and-cheese sandwiches.

I can also remember fishing with some very nice people who were new to the Florida Keys and the local custom of providing lunch for the guides as well. When they broke out their sandwiches, they asked if I wasn't going to take time for lunch too. Rather than embarrass them, I replied, "No, I never eat lunch out on the boat."

From a client's point of view

It is not uncommon to have long-lasting friendships develop between the angler and the guide. I believe this starts with proper courtesy and etiquette toward each other. The angler knows when the guide is working really hard in order to put them into the proper position to make a good cast. This type of fishing is a team effort. You can bet that the angler also knows when they have made a bad cast that possibly spooked the fish, and feels very bad about not holding up their end of the team effort. So, it isn't necessary for the guide to make a sarcastic remark, or worse. It just might be time for the guide to critique the cast in a helpful manner.

It is not only good etiquette, but extremely important for both the angler and guide to know what they expect of each other. Some anglers say that they don't really care whether they catch fish or not. They just want to be out and have a nice day. If that's really true, be sure to let the guide know that before leaving the dock in the morning, because producing fish is normally very important for the guide, who may expect a bit too much of the angler.

Responding to how clients should treat their guides with respect to tipping: Back in my guiding years, I had a client catch a world record fish, along with numerous other large fish, having an overall great day of fishing. The man was extremely excited, and shook my hand with warmth and sincerity when he paid me for my day's guiding. I may have been slightly disappointed at not receiving a tip, along with my daily wages, had not his thanks been so sincere.

Two weeks later, I received a fantastic letter from him, recounting the day's fishing, and thanking me all over again. There was also a check for one hundred dollars in the envelope. He wrote "Thanks for the best day of fishing of my life!" on the lower left portion of the check! Back then, we charged sixty dollars a day.

So, back to the original topic of tipping. If an angler has a great day of fishing (not necessarily catching, which doesn't always happen) and believes that the guide worked hard, and showed them some new things pertaining to the type of fishing they were doing, a 15 to 20 percent tip might be in order. Of course, tipping depends on the financial means of the angler too.

—∞∞∞—

Bob Krumm

Sheridan, Wyoming

Bob Krumm, a regular contributor to *American Angler*, guides on Montana's Bighorn River. The author of three hooks on berries, he is working on a fourth: *The Northwest Berry Book*.

The Guide's Point of View

I've been a fly fishing guide for nearly 20 years. Friends often tell me they couldn't do my job; they couldn't handle being around complaining and pushy people all day. I tell them, "Neither could I, but I'm not around complainers and pushy people most days—I'm usually with people who want to be fishing with me." After all, fishing is supposed to be a pleasurable experience. It's not like going to the doctor or dentist.

The person taking a guided fishing trip usually wants to be out on the water and having a good time. Many of my angling clients have planned for a year or more to come fishing with me. They have a large investment—emotional as well as economic and temporal—in the trip; I have the opportunity, as my friend Michael Maloney puts it, "to be a dream maker." All guides do.

Then why do some of those dreams turn out to be nightmares? Perhaps the angler and the guide have different expectations of their relationship and the fishing trip. False expectations can kill a trip before it ever gets on the water. Unrealistic client expectations get a lot of discussion by guides, but unrealistic guide expectations are as likely to spoil the day.

The Pressure of Numbers

I know guides who feel their sole obligation is to see that their clients catch fish. These guides measure their success by how many fish, or how big a fish, their anglers catch. This type of guide—I call them "numbers" guides—will often nag and ride a client when the fishing is slow and the catch rate isn't up to the guide's standards. A demanding guide makes it tough on the person who wants to enjoy the day and the beauty of the angling environment, wants to savor and appreciate each fish. The numbers guide often will not guide women, children, or beginners because he doesn't want to have a low fish count.

The numbers guide will usually expect his client to be able to cast 40 feet and put the fly on a dime. If the client can't make such a cast, the guide will demand that the client cast again and again until that "dime" is hit. I seldom see such a guide demonstrate the type of cast that needs to be made or teach the client how to make that cast.

Numbers guides sometimes even resort to such unethical practices as the "San Juan shuffle," shuffling upstream of the angler to disturb the bottom and dislodge aquatic invertebrates—chumming more or less. Another practice of numbers guides is to race ahead of the other boats to a hot spot and hold it until the fishing plays out, forcing all other guides and anglers to pass it by.

The Teaching Question

"A guide is a teacher, an instructor, a heck of a lot more than someone who just rows a boat," says fellow Bighorn guide, Gael Larr. "A guide should help to improve a fisherman's casting technique and angling abilities. The mark of a good guide is when a client can go on his or her own and be successful."

I heartily agree with Larr. I can receive no greater compliment than to have a client who fished with me for a day or two go on his or her own and come back and tell me, "You really helped me. I went out yesterday and caught a good number of trout on the techniques you taught me. I couldn't have done it without you."

A good guide will instruct and teach an angler how to fish the waters, what flies to use, and how to improve his or her casting and presentation, but the angler is the one who holds the rod and casts it. It is up to the angler to catch the fish. (Contrary to what you may see on some waters, truly professional guides don't fish while working—we need to devote all our energies to helping our clients.)

Having said all that, I do expect my clients to be able to cast. I don't expect them to be Steve Rajeffs or Joan Wulffs, but I do expect them to be able to make a decent overhead cast. I can, and will if necessary, teach them basic casting, but they can learn quicker, less expensively, and with less frustration away from the river. Most major cities and a lot of smaller towns have fly fishing clubs that provide fly casting classes taught by some of the best casting instructors in the U.S.

Beginners & Experts

A good fishing guide enjoys helping novice fly fishers and delights in their progress. I find that helping a client, beginner or not, improve his or her fishing skills is one of the most important and satisfying things I do.

Sometimes, however, I run into problems with spouses or parents who try too hard to help out. Too often, these expert anglers so badly want their spouses or children to catch a fish that they end up badgering and shouting until the beginner wants nothing to do with fishing. My response to the expert fisher (but inexpert teacher) is, "Please let me take care of Johnny or Susie. You have a chance to fish all day without having to help Johnny or Susie. You fish, and I'll be the guide."

If the expert will let me take over and be the teacher, it usually means that the expert enjoys the day more and gets to fish without interruption. It also means that the expert will have a fishing buddy from then on—precisely what the expert was hoping for.

Respectful Consideration

A guide handles the boat, loads or assists in loading gear, and sets up or prepares lunch, but the guide is not confined to or defined by those menial tasks. The guide is, after all, a skilled professional. Yet, some anglers treat their guides like mere boat rowers or servants.

While not necessarily the world's best fly fisher, the guide nevertheless knows things a more technically expert client doesn't. The guide has fished his or her home waters a long time, in all parts of the season, under many conditions. As a result, the guide knows where the fish are and what they are eating. Whether the guide knows all the casting or fishing techniques in the book is beside the point; but you can darned well bet that he or she knows the techniques that are going to work here and now. To judge a guide's expertise and competence on the vintage or sticker price of the boat, tackle, other equipment, or clothing is to risk insulting the guide and almost guaranteeing a fishless, unpleasant day. I, and all other guides I know, expect to be treated courteously and with respect.

The Old College Try

Realize that a guide can't control much when it comes to fishing—can't make the fish bite, make the wind quit blowing or the rain stop falling, or make high water drop and clear up. But guides do know how to make the most of a lousy deal—if you give them a chance to show you how a pair can sometimes be as good as a full house when it's played properly.

I expect my clients to give each situation a sincere try. I don't expect them to spend the day whining about things beyond their or my control. Every guide hears this from clients: "I can't cast into the wind." The most a guide can do is explain how to cast into the wind and try to teach the angler, but if a whiner gives up after a couple attempts, there isn't much the guide can do to save the day or the week.

Anyone who invests a good deal of money and time on a fishing trip must realize that protecting the investment may mean accepting and adapting to adverse climatic conditions. Complaining about them won't change them or do any good.

The Inquisitive, Happy Client

I expect prospective clients to ask me a lot of questions and to tell me what they expect of me and of the fishing. If we aren't right for each other, I'll say so, and recommend a guide who is better matched to their needs and expectations. The more questions anglers ask, the less likely their, or my, expectations of a good trip will be dashed on the rocks.

Finally, I expect my clients to have a good time. A lot can happen in a day's fishing, but if my anglers and I exchange some jokes, divulge to each other some "secret" patterns, learn a few fishing techniques or master an old one, enjoy the scenery, marvel in the beauty of a fish, appreciate a colorful bird, and are awed by a sunset, we've had a full, rich day—one that will prompt both of us to say, "That was good. Let's do it again, tomorrow or next year."

GEORGE KELLY
Bozeman, Montana

Kelly began guiding on the Snake River in Jackson Hole, Wyoming, in the mid-1960s. He worked for Bud Lilly out of West Yellowstone, guiding on the Henry's Fork and many of the Park rivers. In the '70s he guided independently out of his home in Bozeman, Montana, until moving to the Bighorn River in 1981. He guided and outfitted there until 1989, when he established Bighorn Country Outfitters and the Kingfisher Lodge near Fort Smith, Montana. In 2002, he sold out but continued to guide for the present owners. In 2004, he became head guide for the Firehole Ranch on Hebgen Lake.

Adventure and Misadventure on the Bighorn

*D*espite what you may have heard or read, the Bighorn is remarkably tranquil and free of confrontation for a river of its immense popularity. People generally treat each other with respect, and etiquette is etiquette regardless of where it is practiced. The Bighorn, however, does tend to be crowded at times and opportunities to practice your own brand of etiquette, good or bad, are nearly endless. Not long ago while I was thinking about how to do this short piece about etiquette on the Bighorn, a guest of ours quite coincidentally came to me with this story.

It seems our guest, Lou, who is an angler of average ability but great enthusiasm, was having a tough time taking fish from the piece of water he had selected. A guide whom we will call John happened to notice Lou's dilemma and offered some friendly advice. Not only that, he offered Lou a fly he had tied and suggestions on how Lou should rig his terminal gear. Lou, knowing well that there is no knowledge like local knowledge, took the fly and the advice and to his delight was soon taking the occasional fish. He couldn't help but notice, however, that John and his clients, a couple of hundred yards upstream, were yanking them out with clocklike regularity.

Lou, being a good and conscientious angler, kept his distance, though it was obvious that John and his clients had found the mother lode—a regular cornucopia of the river's goodies. Presently, John motioned for Lou to come upstream, and as Lou got there John loaded his clients into his drift boat and pushed off with the observation that the river gods had smiled on him and his clients, it was time to try elsewhere, and why didn't Lou have a whack at the honey hole. Lou needed no urging and was soon happily catching fish with the same regularity that he had witnessed earlier.

By all rights this story should have a happy ending, but the river gods don't always smile; enter Jim, another guide, but one of quite a different stripe, as we shall see. As mentioned earlier, Lou is an angler of only average skill prone to the usual assortment of backlashes and snarls familiar to us all. He was dealing with one of these, not fishing, but standing in the river where moments earlier he had been casting, when the aforementioned Jim anchored his boat within casting range and proceeded to tell his clients to cast to the same water to which Lou had been casting.

When Lou protested, Jim made the brilliant observation that Lou didn't own the river and since Lou wasn't fishing at that moment he (Jim) had every right to fish it. The appropriate response at this point, in my opinion, would have been a buffalo gun fired at Jim's waterline, but Lou, being a forbearing soul, merely asked Jim his name. Jim, apparently quite proud of himself, refused to give it and, sensing his clients' mounting embarrassment, moved his boat slowly away.

Every guide boat in Montana (if a licensed guide operates it) must display a decal with the guide's license number on it. As Lou approached Jim's boat to try to read this number, Jim canted his boat slightly away so that the number was invisible to Lou, and he drifted off on his ongoing journey down the River Styx.

This story could well end here but it doesn't, for yet another guide across the river had witnessed this happy little encounter and, thoroughly disgusted by it, rowed over and identified Jim for Lou. I don't know what his plans are with the information, but just before he left us, Lou asked me for the address of the Montana Board of Outfitters.

They don't lift guide's licenses for the churlish behavior of people like Jim, nor do they give gold stars for the generosity of spirit manifested in people like John. I don't need to ask whom you would rather meet on the river, nor do I need to ask with whom you would like to be identified. But I will ask, if only to make a point, who do you suppose had the better day on the river, John or Jim, and do you think Lou's day was in any way affected by the people with whom he came in contact? The answers to these questions seem obvious, but think about them a bit before you next venture out on your favorite trout stream. Wouldn't it be something to meet no one but someone like John?

⌘

JOHN A. KUMISKI
Chuluota, Florida

John Kumiski is a fishing guide based in Florida, specializing in the nether reaches of the Indian River. He is also an author: His most recent book is *Fishing Florida's Space Coast*.

Your Guide Deserves Better, or,
Six Ways to Infuriate Your Fly Fishing Guide
From *Salt Water Fly Fishing*, August/September 2000

A Guide's Perspective

*I*t's happened to me more than once. I get up at 4:30 a.m. and drive bleary-eyed to the boat landing while drinking strong, black coffee. I need the caffeine because I want my brain in gear for that 5:30 appointment. I launch my boat and make sure things are in working order. Five-thirty comes and goes. I fight off mosquitoes. I finish my coffee. I watch the sky get light. Six o'clock comes and goes. I fight off mosquitoes. I apply sunscreen. I watch the sun rise. Six-thirty comes. I decide whether to pull the boat out and go home, or go fishing alone, since the charter isn't showing up. I spend time wishing I had gotten a deposit. This is a worst-case scenario, but it happens to all fishing guides.

That's why most of us ask for deposits. If you really want to make a fishing guide miserable, here are some other ideas you can put into play, or do the contrary, for those of you who are more conscientious about the fate of your fellow human beings.

Show Up Late

What better way to get the day off on the wrong foot than to show up 20 or 30 minutes late? If you want the guide in the best possible spirits, however, show up a couple of minutes early and be ready to go right at the appointed time.

Bring Noisemakers

In my boat, I really dislike drinks of any kind in cans. They always spill and the empties roll around and make noise. Drinks for boats need to have screw tops on them to help prevent spills. In a boat, plastic drink containers work much better than glass bottles or aluminum cans. Rattling around in a cooler full of ice and water also makes noise. And dropping that cooler lid produces a big thud. Fish in shallow water are very vulnerable and stay on the alert, sensitive to every sound and shadow. Making these kinds of fish scaring sounds, especially when the guide is trying to stalk some fish, will surely drive him nuts.

The Premature Castoff

It's always enjoyable when an eager-to-go fisherman unties the boat from the dock and jumps aboard, muddying the deck with dirty shoes and casting us out into the current before the engine is started. Before the boat leaves the dock certain chores need to be performed. I prefer for all gear to be stowed and the motor to be started and warmed up before I ask my anglers aboard. Yes, a passenger should always wait to be asked aboard a boat, or they should ask for permission to come aboard.

Dirty Up the Deck

"A clean boat is a happy boat," says Florida Keys guide Nat Ragland. I agree. I want my boat to stay as clean as possible during a day's fishing. I put a towel down on the deck so everyone can clean their shoes. Sand and dirt abrades fly lines and flies into your face while the boat is running at speed. Shoes with black bottoms make black scuff marks that are very difficult to remove from the deck surface. A scrub brush, some bleach (or sometimes a solvent), some serious elbow grease, and quite a bit of time are needed to eliminate these marks. Most guides prefer that their anglers wear shoes that have white bottoms, which boat and fishing shoes always have.

Tote Your Tubes

Fly rods cost some serious money, and we all carry them in tubes to protect them. But I have never seen anyone use one of these tubes while actually fishing. In my 16-foot skiff, there is no place to store rod tubes, and I don't want them in my boat. Step on a rod tube while fighting a fish and there's a very real possibility that the fish will be lost, and that the rod and perhaps some bones will be broken. Leave rod tubes in the car when you go fishing.

Hook Your Guide

Once out on the water when we're actually looking for fish, I instruct new anglers on what to look for, how to see fish, and how to present the fly. As part of this conversation, I introduce the clock system, by which I give casting directions. During our discussion I explain that if fish are seen between 12 o'clock and 3 o'clock (for a right-handed caster), the fisherman must either cast backhanded, left-handed, or wait for me to turn the boat before casting. Otherwise they'll hook me or other boat occupants. I get hooked all the time. I accept getting hooked as an occupational hazard. I don't like getting hooked, though, and I don't know many other guides who like it, either. I realize that it happens to everyone sooner or later (I've hooked two guides myself), but please try to be careful for the sake of the guy with the push pole. He'll work better when he's not concerned about his personal safety.

The above situations have happened to me during real-life adventures aboard my Dolphin skiff. Some of these situations occur frequently. (Names were withheld to protect the perpetrators.) Guides don't expect their fishermen to have the eyes of an osprey and the casting skill of Steve Rajeff. But they do expect some common sense and common courtesy from their clients. If you don't make your guide miserable, you'll have a more productive day and both of you will have more fun. And fun on the water is really what saltwater fly fishing is all about.

Communication is key.

—∞∞∞—

Smith Coleman
Fredericksburg, Virginia

Coleman teaches the Discovery Program, an outdoor education curriculum for Orange County public schools. He also serves as chairman of the executive committee for Friends of the Rappahannock. Smith guides a few clients a year on the Rappahannock for smallmouth, shad, and rockfish.

Guiding the Masses

The second phone call came at 5:00 p.m. at my fly shop in Fredericksburg, Virginia. The guy said he had talked some friends into coming along on the trip, and was that OK? I was nice and said, "sure, fine," and all that, but I thought I knew the second question: "How much will it cost each of us if I bring five people?"

I ignored the question like Kennedy ignored the first message from the Kremlin. I said, "I can handle six, but it's pushing it." Then I said, "No more." He heard the skirt and said nice things about me for a long time. Then he asked again.

I gave him a better price, and said, "No less."

The price was right, and he knew it, and I knew it, so he said nice things about me, and we hung up.

The third call came after 9:00 p.m. the next night at my home. "I've got eight people," he said. And he excused himself and apologized for a long time, and said nice things about me. Things he'd heard and read.

Guiding a group—avoid fishing too close.

I was mad now because the job I had to do got more difficult exponentially every time we added a person. He went to the price not knowing I was mad. I came down again, and said, "No more people, no less money." He said nice things because he could tell I was mad.

They showed up at the Rappahannock in minivans and 4x4s. I stood in the parking area near the Route 1 Bridge with my waders on, and watched the procession.

I had been up since 12:30 the night before grading essays, and I had taught all day. These guys were down from D.C. to get in an afternoon of shad fishing on the Rap with me, and I couldn't help but sense that they knew—they had to—that I was hungry, that I was a teacher and that therefore, I would take what I could get as a guide and be thankful. But maybe it was my mood.

They introduced themselves starting with the caller/pricer, and went around the semi-circle until I counted nine people.

I said, "Get your waders on and line up your rods," and walked back to my Subaru to get some flies—but really to get away before I lost it.

I stood at the car thinking about a cigarette I wanted but could never have again as long as I lived, and I watched them pull piles of gear and rods and a dog out of the vehicles.

What was it they expected? Was I going to be able to do the things I do well for these people? Self-doubt crept into my psyche. I saw tangled lines, people in water over their heads, fish killed. It was all ugly.

Suddenly I was struck with the knowledge of what I would do, how I would go about guiding nine people and a Labrador retriever. I was not mad anymore. I was the best guide these boys had ever dreamed of, and I would take no shit.

I walked up and saw the caller/pricer drop a cigarette butt in the sand and told him to dress his butts.

"What?" he said.

"Dress it," I said. "Tear it in half so it won't sit there for two years."

He looked at me, and I could tell he was about to realize that there were nine of him and one of me; so I said, "I'll never remember any of your names, but none of you is named Bill, so when I want your attention I'll say 'Bill,' and that means every-body listen. Got it?"

They all stopped.

"The shad will be here in about a half an hour, and I want everyone in place and fishing before then." I pulled out my fly box and gave over a handful of Chesapeake Shad Flies, an old-timey pattern I had grabbed from a bin in my shop. I said, "I'll post each of you on the river, and you'll all catch fish. Lots of fish."

"Let's get leaders on. 0x is fine—won't spook these fish; 3x is too light because stripers are behind the shad. If I tell you to change flies it means the stripers are here, and I'll have to move some of you to a different spot. The dog needs a leash."

There was a long silence, and I rocked back on my heels and held the incredulous stares of my clients. Then they all started to gear up, and I petted the dog.

We marched in twos down to the river and no one said much. I placed the first guy and started to walk on when he said, "There's almost no water here. It's a foot deep." I turned around and looked at him and everyone stopped. "The tide's coming in," I said. "The fish will be on it." Then I turned and walked, pointing out the next spot.

I strung them out in a pattern I had seen the local fishermen make. On the ninth guy I turned around and started back up the line.

"Everyone pinch their barbs," I yelled. They all stopped and looked at me. "You won't need them," I yelled, "These fish will be thick, and I don't want to kill two hundred shad this afternoon." They pinched barbs and started casting.

I stopped at the next fisherman and watched his cast. "You've got a hell of a tailing loop," I said. He stopped casting and said, "What?"

"A tailing loop," I said. "Turn your body toward me and stick your left foot forward. Watch your back cast. Now apply even pressure to your stroke; you've been snapping your wrist and it takes the rod out of plane. It won't work here. You'll have four wind knots in half an hour, and when the stripers come they'll break you off." I waited till he had tried it, and moved on.

I kept an eye on the river below us for the tentative swirls of shad. I watched the horizon for the nightly flights from the lower Rappahannock of great blue herons and ospreys. They all came at once. I saw fish three hundred yards away as they rolled on the incoming tide. The birds came in, the herons placing themselves on rocky outposts, and the ospreys hovering and diving.

"Fish are here," I said. "Keep those lines wet." Ten minutes later, three of the sports had fish on.

For two hours the fishing picked up, and then it died. I yelled, "Hey Bill," and everyone turned to look. "Change flies," I said. "Stripers are next." They reeled in like crazy and dug for Clousers and Deceivers in their vests.

I told three guys to follow me and walked them across a deep run to an island. "Fish out and across," I said. "Your takes will happen at the end of the swing. Set the hook first, hard, then stick your rod out at a right angle and fight from the butt, not the tip. Yell 'fish on' so the guy below you can get out of your way. Keep the fish off the bank and only raise your tip if you think he's wallowing in rocks at the bottom. Net the fish for each other and do it from below, not above, because you'll spook him, and he'll break off. Release these fish with lots of care. Don't just plunk them back in; they'll die if you do. Got it?"

"Yeah," they all said.

I told them I'd be back when I heard "fish on" to place someone else where the last one had been, and we'd keep a fish going that way.

I walked back to the others and posted them.

Clouds had moved in and conditions looked perfect for stripers. I worked hard at placement, watching the casts and centering their efforts in deeper runs that the fish would move in on. I rigged an in-line pair of flies for some of the guys, leading off with a Clouser and trailing with a shad fly to get the rig down in the water column.

"Fish on," we heard, and we turned to see the lowest man on

the island with his rod bowed and the tip stuck straight up in the air.

"Get that tip down," I yelled. He dropped his tip and stuck it at a right angle. It was a good fish, and he went into the backing with long runs in the current.

"Fish on," another one yelled, and he stuck his rod out at a right angle. This fish was smaller and the guy played him quickly and pulled him to the bank before the first fish had been netted.

They caught stripers until after sunset, and then it died.

"It's over for a half an hour," I said. "Stripers won't hunt again until full dark. I'm for staying here because I think there will be some fifteen-pounders tonight."

In the dying light we regrouped. I handed out black flies and explained that stripers hunt silhouettes at night, and black shows up better than white. I got a few skeptical looks, but they tied on the flies.

The Rappahannock sunset fastened winter hues of pink and gold to the April sky. The guys were grinning and laughing, and I was having fun. "Get that dog," I said. "He can swim for a while."

We played with the dog on the bank until full dark, then leashed him on the bank. The guys walked out to the water and fished another hour. They caught more fish, but no fifteen-pounders.

I called it at 9:45, and we walked back to the cars. Everyone paid up and tipped well, and we said our good-byes. The caller/pricer walked over to my car and said nice things and I thanked him. He was really very nice, and I liked him again. He said he'd call again next spring and I said fine.

"Bring 'em on," I said. "The more people, the more fish."

I guided the striper and shad run another half-dozen times

and never did as well. It was a good shad year all told, but the stripers never really turned on.

I've thought a lot about that day. I bet those guys have too. The "Bill" thing was overboard, and I'm sure they've laughed about it. But I know they learned a ton, and the truth is that next spring, they won't need me to catch fish.

Lori-Ann Murphy
Victor, Wyoming

Lori-Ann Murphy founded Reel Women Fly Fishing Adventures in 1994. It was the first company to offer "women only" trips all over the world. Lori-Ann's home waters are in Idaho and Wyoming near Jackson Hole, where she fishes and guides on the South Fork of the Snake River. Lori-Ann worked as the fly fishing consultant for Meryl Streep and Kevin Bacon in *The River Wild*, accompanied Martha Stewart in the Wyoming wilderness for four days of camping and fishing for a feature article, and competed in both the 2001 and 2002 ESPN Great Outdoor Games.

A Touch of Class

There is a rhythm to guiding fly fishermen. The rules are learned early in a guide's career only to be transformed. Each experience becomes a tutor for personal as well as professional expression. While the weather and fishing conditions are important in finding fish, it is really the people that define the day.

Don Harvey and Jim Fish had been fishing together for close to fifty years when I first met them. They are from Alberta, Canada, Bow River country. Hearing of the thick hatches of *tricos* on the Colorado, they booked a week at the lodge I was working that summer. The lodge held twelve guests, most of whom had only been fishing a few years. I had been assigned to work with these splendid gentlemen for a full week in late September.

Sometimes you meet people that stop you in your tracks and you're not sure why, but you find yourself paying attention. I noticed their excitement as they stood looking at the unrestrained Colorado River. The high country desert filled with the smell of sage was familiar territory, but this was their first time to cast a fly on the Colorado. Stories of other rivers were being exchanged as I tried to prepare for the day. The sound of questions followed by chuckles. Words of respect toward one another rang loudly to me. I felt their silent stares as they watched me run around the truck five times making sure I didn't forget anything. Mostly I was working hard at staying focused. As a rookie guide I did not possess the quiet grace of river years under my belt. These were experienced fishermen and I was nervous. When I did slow down, I found myself rooted in new ground.

Don Harvey has spent his life working his family's ranch and oil business, and possesses the natural refinement of a great businessman. He has a way of selecting the perfect question to make one think beyond their normal boundaries. Jim Fish is the quintessential bachelor. Jim wears a bow tie to dinner and sparkles when he refers to his fly fishing library. His collection includes several first editions from the great authors of the world of fly fishing. It was Jim who told me to read Roderick Haig-Brown. This was just one of the many gifts he shared with me. Together, Don and Jim work as philanthropists endowing special projects, which will help their community. They laugh all the time.

New-sprung guides to any operation usually work with novice fishermen. This is just one of the guide rules. It makes sense because usually, new guides have more patience and are very excited about teaching. The guides with more experience offer their expertise about the area, and possess a fine skill of telling people what they can expect. Only an experienced guide can get away with lines like, "You should have been here yesterday." Given some situations the guest may hear, "You should have been here fifteen years ago!" In any case, this was one of the few times I had ever guided experienced fishermen. I knew I would be the one learning.

They told me from the start that they preferred dry fly fishing. In the next sentence they told me their favorite fly was the Royal Wulff. I knew they were excited to fish the *trico* hatch, but I was puzzled about their favorite fly. Delicate small flies needed to imitate the *tricos* did not match up with the style of their preferred pattern. I like the Royal Wulff myself. It is a wonderful attractor pattern used to imitate several aquatic insects. The red thread wrapped around peacock herl drives fish crazy. Small dry flies can be difficult to see so the white wings of the Royal Wulff become a great benefit when you are intensely staring at the water. I had used them in a size 12 primarily to see if I could bring fish to the surface of a suspecting piece of water. I would never have thought of using this fly during a *trico* hatch. My everyday personality would be to tell these guys they were nuts, but I stayed quiet.

The start of the *trico* hatch filled the crisp early morning air. Tiny black-and-white mayflies were gradually lifting off from the river's surface. We gathered ourselves along the bank and looked into the river. Water that had just been quiet started to stir as fish heads gently broke the surface. We could see the red sides flash at us as sixteen- to twenty-inch rainbows woke up to the morning feed.

"This is a job for the Royal Wulff," Don exclaimed. Jim smiled and opened his box revealing their favorite pattern in several sizes. The smallest was a size 16. I felt we needed a much smaller fly, say a size 20. They saw my puzzled face and kindly asked if I would help them by stringing up my rod with one of their flies. Tying on their own flies, they were off. Another guide rule is that clients fish, not guides. I followed orders in preparing my fly rod. When I looked up I heard the splashing of a nice trout as it reached Don's net. Just upstream from Don, I saw Jim's rod bent and a smile that reached the outer limits of his face. They were catching fussy fish feeding on small mayflies with something that looked like it could knock the fish out with the wrong cast!

I appeased them by having my fly rod prepared, but I did not fish. When I fish, I go into my own world, and I have a difficult time paying attention to anything else. My nerves were just starting to relax and I was able to appreciate the company of two men enjoying their favorite passion.

It is not often you find such kindred spirits in a place of work. I had left my nursing career to follow a ruling passion not knowing what life would look like down the road. The choice to learn more about the rivers of the Rocky Mountain West and the fish in them was found in the world of guiding. I was overwhelmed with the giddy feelings that replaced the frozen fear that I had felt only hours earlier. Don and Jim had been fishing together longer than my lifetime and they were acting like they were young boys. A common theme in most of their jokes mentioned McClelland's Scotch. As far as I could tell, this was the only factor which revealed their age. I was completely satiated as I watched them bring several more fat rainbows to their nets. In my guide position, it was all I could do to run from one to the other trying to help them land fish, exclaiming, "Nice fish." They fished the entire hatch, which lasted a few hours, with the same fly.

As the morning warmed into midday, the hatch started to thin. Don and Jim had meticulously covered the water, finding most of the fish they were after. All were released and set free to find safer feeding water. It was time for a break, but I felt I should show these men every piece of water I knew that held some of my pet fish. I was excited to share my secrets. "OK, let's go, we have more water to cover!" We were wade fishing and so it was necessary to cover a lot of ground to get to the other sections of river. We were all wearing neoprene waders, and it was hot from a bright sun burning through the dry mountain air.

A constant buzz of the river followed my steps as I glided over logs and boulders. I was pushing a pretty good pace when I heard Don yell, "Nanny, I've already had one heart attack, I don't plan on having another today." Jim's laughter carried over the river's roar. Apparently, they had decided to call me "Nanny Long Legs" for my bossy nature and six feet.

So we stopped. The river made a large bend, a place I had used to cross several times while moving upstream. Shade from the old cottonwood and aspens in peaking colors of red and yellow made for a perfect rest site. We ate, took naps (another rule broken), and woke up to an incredible caddis hatch in an area I had never fished. The Royal Wulff finished out the day.

Back at the lodge, everyone started in on the day's report. "How big, how many, and what did you catch them on . . . ?" These are the conversations where guides are named heroes or zeros. A liar's den so to speak. Most of the anglers at the lodge were beginners. Numbers of fish seem to be important validation for working the rod, line, and fly. Some anglers may catch several trout and feel it wasn't enough, while others experience a total sense of bliss having landed one fish. In any case, everyone was anxious to hear from Don and Jim.

I've retold their stories. They fished a time when river exploration took on a whole new meaning. They fished the Dean River in British Columbia in the 1930s. Flying in with a float plane, they had to use a chain saw to cut trees so they could turn the plane around when they decided to leave. They fished for days until all their supplies were gone and until every dream was saturated from some fish puzzle. Numerous giant steelhead on dry flies. They fished this area for many years before they ever saw another fishing soul.

They have seen a lot of change over the years, but you will never hear them complain when it comes to fishing. Sure, they seek those far and away places that hold secrets. Fishing is their life passion. But they are also content to fish their beloved Bow River always learning from home water. They have a lot to brag about, but I have never heard them do so. Don Harvey and Jim Fish are content taking in the day and unfolding the mystery on any fishing stream. Validation is just being there. The challenge is to continue the search and keep the sparkle alive by learning new tricks.

I learned how one fly could be used in a variety of conditions and how important it is to be open to new ideas. These guys could have gone back to the lodge and had everyone hanging on their boasting words, but that would not have made anyone feel any better about their day. The very brief report that they did give allowed the other guests to tell their tales: frustration, losing fish, and, for some, finally catching Mr. Big Rainbow.

In the years to follow, I've continued to learn from Don and Jim. They followed me up to Jackson, Wyoming, and never stopped using a Royal Wulff. They quizzed me on tales from Roderick Haig-Brown.

Another toast, McClelland's held high. "We had a great day."

Part Five

SALMON AND STEELHEAD

"Fishing manners, like social customs, are subject to change. In the last forty years, salmon fishing has changed more than in the previous century. The number of salmon anglers has grown rapidly and promises to continue its growth as long as there is room for more salmon anglers to crowd in."

—Lee Wulff

CHARLES PHAIR
New Brunswick, Canada

Phair's *Atlantic Salmon Fishing*, originally published by The Derrydale Press in 1937, is still considered the best book on Atlantic-salmon fishing ever published. Heir to a Maine starch fortune, Phair devoted his adult life to salmon fishing throughout the world. His expertise included fishing the wet fly, fishing the dry fly, tackle, flies and their uses, casting, weather, and spawning. His home territory was New Brunswick—the Tobique, the Kedgwick, the Cascapedia, and the Restigouche. His season was long; he fished nearly every day of it for decades. He knew his salmon.

Protecting and Stocking Salmon Rivers
From *Atlantic Salmon Fishing*, Derrydale Press, 1937

Etiquette and Customs

*I*f you have leased fishing on a river with which you are not familiar, it is well to get in touch with the superintendent of the club, if there is one, and to find out from him what it is customary to do about not only your fishing but many other things as well. Clubs on the different rivers establish certain customs it is well to follow, since your guides and others in your employ will naturally expect you to do so. My first year on the Restigouche, I fished from a Gaspé boat, which requires two men. The day I arrived I wanted to cross over to an island in front of the camp, only about seventy-five yards away, with just an ordinary quiet piece of water between. Going down to the river where one of my guides was at the boat, I asked him to set me over on the island, which he said he would do just as soon as he could find the other man. He wouldn't put me across on that island, though he could have easily enough, because it was not the custom for one man to handle a Gaspé boat.

On some rivers, even if your lodge is only a small one and there is no one fishing from it but yourself, the chances are that your cook will want someone to help him and to wait on the table; and he will expect you to supply the camp with the same sort of foodstuffs the club camp has, and any number of other things, too numerous to mention. But if one follows club ideas, everything will go on more smoothly; and as the club is in a position to do you a great many favors if it sees fit, it is well to follow along in its footsteps.

A mail-boat service such as is maintained on the Restigouche is very convenient; the men bring not only the mail for the Lodge but any small packages, and on the trip down take fish to be shipped. A tag bearing the name and address is tied through the fish's mouth, and when it reaches Matapedia it is boxed and iced before shipping. Manzer Howard, who was guiding me, once stuffed a lot of sheet lead down the throat of one of my fish, to beat the weight of a fish killed by a certain member of my party, and when we shipped the fish down river by the mail boat that particular one was addressed to the late Ezra Fitch. Two weeks later I had a letter from Mr. Fitch thanking me for the fish, and asking, "why the hell all the sheet lead in him."

There is one thing which must never be forgotten, provided you may ever want to go fishing again, and that is to tip the cook, guides, mail-boat man and what other help you have had. It does not necessarily have to be a large amount, since it is really a way of showing them that you appreciate the many things they have done for you during your stay.

Above all, don't forget that a guide is a guide and a cook a cook. The guide takes care of your fishing tackle, looks after his boat, and handles it for you while you are fishing. The cook cooks for anyone who may be at the camp. Don't ask either of them to run errands and to do things that are out of their line. If you do, they won't like it.

An instance of how much guides and cooks will stand before blowing up is the case of one of my guides, who was once doing the guiding and cooking for a fisherman. The first morning Jack brought in fried eggs and bacon for the man's breakfast; the gentleman allowed he did not want his eggs fried, but boiled, so Jack took them back to the kitchen and boiled some. Next morning, naturally thinking he preferred boiled eggs, Jack cooked them that way, but that morning he wanted them fried. For dinner one night Jack served canned beans; the man wanted to know what brand they were. Jack said he didn't remember, having thrown the can away, whereupon he was told to go find the can, which he did; when Jack returned with the tin, the gentleman said he did not like that brand at all and told Jack to heat up a different one. This went on for a week, until one morning for breakfast Jack brought in the fry pan full of beans; when the man saw them, he told Jack he did not want his beans in the fry pan. And Jack replied, "You are going to get them in the fry pan whether you want them or not," and brought the pan down over the man's head, beans and all.

Joan Salvato Wulff
Lew Beach, New York

A native of New Jersey, Joan Salvato was a tournament caster from 1937 to 1960, winning one International and seventeen National titles, including the 1951 Fisherman's Distance event against all-male competition. She has the distinction of casting a fly 161 feet in a registered tournament! Joan still holds the International Women's Fishing Association records for brook trout and Atlantic salmon.

An active member of the Outdoor Writer's Association of America, Joan is also the author of *Joan Wulff's Fly Casting Techniques; Fly Fishing: Expert Advice from a Woman's Perspective;* and *Fly Casting Accuracy.*

In 1994, she was voted Angler of the Year and appeared on the cover of *Fly Rod & Reel* magazine, for whom she writes a regular casting column. Joan has starred in numerous videos, the most recent the unprecedented 1997 *Dynamics of Fly Casting.*

The Etiquette of Atlantic Salmon Fishing

I love Atlantic salmon fishing for many reasons, but primarily because these magnificent fish can be caught on trout tackle. And, because they are on a spawning run, there's the challenge of presenting flies to fish that aren't feeding.

There have never been, nor will there ever be, enough fish or rivers to satisfy the needs of salmon anglers and so, there is a need for specific angling etiquette. Salmon fishing is a sport in which social convention has prescribed rules.

If the water is privately held, the number of rods allowed to fish at one time will be fixed. The river is divided into "beats"— a beat being a suitable section of river in which salmon will lie. Rules are set for either one or two anglers to fish the beat. On certain rivers (the Grand Cascapedia in Quebec is one) only one angler may fish at a time, and so time becomes the equitable way to share turns, with anglers changing places, say, every thirty minutes.

Traditionally, salmon fishermen make one or two casts across the current, letting the fly swing under tension until it has reached a position directly below. Then a step or two is taken downstream and the presentation is repeated. With two anglers, one starts at the head of the pool and the other halfway down. When the lead angler finishes the pool, he or she then goes to the head of the pool, covering the water that their companion has fished. Each tries not to monopolize a given section, moving downstream at a reasonable rate, unless one angler raises a salmon and wants to work on it for awhile. In this case, the other may go around and continue to fish below.

Boat fishing is necessary on large, unwadable rivers, and here the etiquette rules are that anglers take turns covering the water on each "drop." The boat is anchored and the angler presents his fly in a systematic pattern so that it will be seen by every salmon in the surrounding water. The anchor is then lifted and the boat (usually a canoe) drifts downstream to the next drop.

Good manners dictate that turns are taken from a boat by whoever starts fishing on each successive session or each day, or who takes the heads or tails of pools that are waded.

The salmon get some consideration too; at lodges it is traditional for pools to be rested in the afternoons, with the fishing resuming in early evening and lasting until dark. This works pretty well, and the lodge guides can make sure the sports play by the rules.

However, there is one thing that bothers me, which probably falls under the heading of "integrity." Salmon camps keep logs of daily catches. Many guests are beginners and cannot cast well enough to cover the salmon lies efficiently. Consequently, the guide will suggest, or the sport will ask, that the guide "finish out the drop." The guide becomes the fisherman, until he hooks a salmon; then the rod is handed back to the sport, who lands the fish. Back at camp the catch is entered in the log as having been caught by the sport. This practice is traditional and has consequences: the lack of truth in the records. Which anglers truly hooked and landed their salmon? Which were hooked by the guide? I have no problem with the scenario as it occurs, whatever gives the angler pleasure. However, I would draw the line with the record book. Both names should be listed.

On public water, an equitable system kicks in when anglers outnumber casting spots. Anglers work down the pool, with about two cast's lengths between them. Again, if an angler raises a fish and chooses to make more than three casts from the same spot, the waiting upstream angler may go below him. Although, when I've raised a fish and can't get it to take in a few casts, I feel guilty and usually move downstream, allowing the next angler to try for "my" fish. I think local convention would rule here.

When the angler reaches the bottom of the pool, he or she leaves the water and waits in line until it is their turn to start at the head again. It has been my experience that a nice camaraderie develops among anglers in that waiting period, often with lots of fishing tales shared.

Unfortunately, sometimes things can get sticky. There are stories of anglers arriving at a pool well before it is legal to fish, and securing a stand on a rock or other landmark thought to offer the best chance of hooking a salmon. They don't move from that spot all day, except perhaps to have a friend take over while they take a break. Tempers flare in such instances and well they should; this is a breech of etiquette in that there is no fair sharing. It's first come/first served.

In the 23 years that Lee and I fished together we always

adhered to the rules very strictly. If we shared by time, we'd change positions right on the button. When people are emotionally involved it is easy to start fudging on the time and it can get out of hand if both are passionate anglers. If the time is yours to give, you can give it, but don't let it be taken. It's like the old adage, "Good fences good neighbors make." Enjoy!

LEE WULFF
1905–1991

Charles Kurault said, "Lee Wulff was to fishing what Einstein was to physics."

Engineer, artist, inventor, poet, and author, Lee also filmed, produced, edited, and was featured in many segments for ABC's *American Sportsman* and CBS's *Sports Spectacular.* He also produced angling videos and films for various private and governmental organizations worldwide.

Lee Wulff was a founding member of the Federation of Fly Fishers and was also President of the Canadian Atlantic Salmon Federation. He was singularly the most significant pioneer in the study and conservation of the Atlantic salmon.

In the 1930s, Lee Wulff was already drawn to a unique concept: Rather than hooking and killing fish, why not return them, unharmed, to the water, for someone else to catch? He has been called by many the father of catch-and-release fishing, and in 1936 he gave to the fishing world the powerful phrase, "A good game fish is too valuable to be caught only once." In 1967, Lee married casting champion Joan Salvato.

In 1991, during a recertification for his pilot's license, at the age of eighty-six, Lee Wulff had a massive heart attack while at the controls of his plane. An era was over.

Manners in Fishing for Atlantic Salmon
From *The Atlantic Salmon*, The Lyons Press, 1983

Fishing manners, like social customs, are subject to change. In the last forty years, salmon fishing has changed more than in the previous century. The number of salmon anglers has grown rapidly and promises to continue its growth as long as there is room for more salmon anglers to crowd in.

Three decades ago, it was rare to have to share a pool, even on waters open to the public. Now it is a problem to find a place to step in between casting anglers, where one can both reach a fish and not tangle with other lines. There are pools where, in order to fish, an angler must join a procession of men who have spaced themselves a short distance apart and who move, continually casting, down through the pool to its tail, where each one returns to the head of the pool to start through it again. There are other pools where an angler simply seeks a station from which he can reach a salmon and stays there until his fishing time is done, for there is no other nearby water left for him to fish.

In view of such conditions, it is difficult to advise on mannerly conduct. What happens to the dry-fly angler who wants to fish upstream while three wet-fly anglers are taking turns working their way down the pool? How long should a fisherman cast to a fish he has raised, when several others are fishing toward him? Should he make them go around him, or should he give up on the fish and move on down the pool? Answers to these and related questions would try the wisdom of Solomon.

Where an angler wades with relation to the salmon is important not only to himself but to other anglers who may be interested in fishing the same waters. Salmon frequently lie in water of wading depth at the side of deep pools instead of near their centers. A wading angler may, unknowingly, disturb these fish, causing them to move off into deeper water where they will be much harder to attract with a fly. Where an angler is fishing completely alone, the only damage is to the angler's own fishing, but where other anglers may be interested in fishing the same waters, either simultaneously or in sequence, it is damaging to their fishing, as well. Canoes or boats, especially those equipped with outboard motors, often disturb the fishing in a pool.

These situations are far more frequent than one might suppose. Anglers who do not know the pools well, or are strangers to the river, often, out of ignorance, wade where the fish would normally be lying, and fish where they normally would not. If an angler is fishing strange water without a guide, it would be a courteous thing for him to ask local fishermen near whom he is fishing, whether the path on which he plans to wade the pool will disturb the salmon or affect their fishing. The question will serve two purposes: prevent him from the possibility of spoiling their opportunities and will result, in most cases, in their pointing out to him just where the fish are most likely to be.

Etiquette on the salmon river depends upon the locality and the situation. The angler who can conform to the local pattern will create the least inconvenience.

My hope is that you, gentle reader, find salmon fishing where you may spend your fishing hours with salmon beneath your fly and no one else impatient to get at them, where you will have time to fish thoughtfully for a fish and come back to fish for him again the following day. Unless you can do these things, you will never know quite how thrilling salmon fishing can be. I hope if we meet, we shall so share the fishing that neither of us shall have any regrets as a result.

CLAUDE M. KREIDER
Long Beach, California

Kreider fished the entire Pacific coast from Mexico to Washington State in search of fresh- and saltwater fish. His favorite species to fish for in latter years were yellowtail and albacore. He liked to make his own tackle, and was a contributor to many outdoor magazines. He authored *Steelhead* and *Making Rods*, and he was editor of *Western Outdoors* in Southern California for many years.

The Steelhead Angler's Attitude and Ethics
From *Steelhead*, G. P. Putnam & Sons, 1948

It is unfortunate that many anglers will recognize the necessity of conservation measures in regard to the various fresh water trout species but will not accept the premise that steelhead should have the same protective measures, such as smaller daily bag limits, curtailed fishing seasons, and perhaps certain closed areas during the spawning run. Several understandable factors seem to account for this unfortunate wide divergence of opinion in respect to the two classes of trout. After all, both the sea-run and landlocked fish are affected by a combination of conditions much similar, at least insofar as perpetuation of the species is concerned.

But there is little publicity given the steelhead from the conservation angle, and few constructive thoughts have been disseminated materially to educate the angler and change his viewpoint. He thinks of the great steelhead schools fresh in from salt water as a natural and regular occurrence. They have always appeared in their native river at the appointed time. The ocean is large, and food is ample, so like the great schools of tuna and albacore and salmon, which are also migratory, the steelhead runs will be perpetual, they have always arrived on time and always will. But this is faulty reasoning and not based upon even cursory examination of the matter.

It is easier to appreciate the problems that affect the landlocked trout: increased heavy fishing; drought and increased use of water for power and irrigation throughout the West, lowering to the danger point many trout waters; pollution; forest fires and the clearing of land, which permit too-rapid runoff of the rains and serious erosion of stream beds and silting of the spawning bars. These conditions are well-known to the average angler. Every summer fishing season he can observe the harm done. And each year he knows that millions of young trout are artificially propagated and planted by his state fish commission or other constituted authority. Thus he recognizes the need of conservation measures affecting landlocked trout.

But too seldom does the angler realize that all the above dangerous conditions also affect the steelhead. This seagoing rainbow of course lives most of its adult life in the ocean, but the spawning fish must reach the gravel bars far upriver; the eggs must have favorable conditions for hatching; and the baby trout, for their first year of life in the river, are as adversely affected by unnatural conditions in the stream as are similar small fish in landlocked waters.

With the steelhead run considered ample and perpetual by the unthinking angler, he does not see the necessity of curtailing the legal daily bag limit of the steelhead, nor will he accept a shorter fishing season along with closure of certain waters to protect the migrating fish on the spawning beds or before they reach them. Thus the reasoning of many anglers may be entirely unselfish but faulty. They have not thought the matter through. Then there is another class who claim to believe in conservation but want it applied only to the other fellow. And far too many do think along these selfish lines, although I like to believe that they are a small minority.

And as we examine a cross-section of the angling fraternity here in the West, we at once find the ordinary sportsman, whose numbers are legion. He believes in our fish and game laws and so is law abiding. He stops with his daily bag limit, as prescribed, and observes the closure of fishing waters. But if he is permitted, say, his five steelhead a day, he proposes to get them if possible. Thus, of winter steelhead, he might easily, and legally, kill fifty pounds of fish each day. Of these perhaps more than half will be females carrying upward of 3,500 eggs each, and they will be almost ready to spawn in many instances.

One such ten-pound fish will provide sufficient food for several meals; another might properly be saved for a special friend; and there may be an unusual occasion, such as the opening day, when a full legal limit might permissibly be killed. But the thinking angler who believes in real conservation will keep his one or two of these great winter travelers and release the other fish after they have been properly subdued. After all, it is presumably the thrill of hooking and fighting to a sporty finish these silvery warriors that has led the angler afield. His pride is satisfied; he has taken his limit. All the fish do not have to be displayed to prove his prowess.

Careful handling does not in the least harm the steelhead that are to be released. That point has been well proven. We have only to observe egg-taking operations at any fish hatchery, where hundreds of brood fish are handled daily and held firmly in the hands for stripping without the least harm to them. And aside from the purely conservation phase of returning to the water a fish that is not needed, I submit that there is real satisfaction, and fine sportsmanship, in thus releasing that gamy, battling steelhead, which has fought nobly to the last gasp. It is a gesture of admiration and respect to a worthy antagonist.

A defensive thought will arise in the minds of many anglers

that, after all, our fishing regulations are promulgated by the authorities, who should know, and often after consultation with organized sportsmen's groups. This plan is practiced by the Fish and Game Commission of California at present and is a sound healthy policy. Aside from the broadminded and human desire to sit down and hear the sportsman's views, there is the practical premise that law evasion is better prevented by education and mutual understanding than by attempting to enforce regulations with which the thinking sportsman is not in accord.

So much for this desired cooperation and how it works in theory. Sportsmen's conservation organizations do accomplish a great deal of good; their basic policy is sound, and most of their members are sincere. But too often a selfish group, an organized and noisy minority, will take the lead and work only for their own selfish interests to the detriment of any real conservation attempt.

The "meat-getter" will take his daily limit if possible and kill them, perhaps cast the fish up into the brush if they are not needed, for there is no one to see. And there is a type of angler who does just that. Again some men always hoping for a larger fish will hastily tear the hook from the little fellow and throw him back in a hurry to try again for a better one. And they think of themselves as sportsmen!

The deliberate snagging of fish by the use of multiple hook lures is of course reprehensible and illegal, but it is often done by men who lack any vestige of real sporting instinct. Again it is the personal code rather than the tackle, which is important.

Sporting ethics entail consideration of other anglers in these days of heavily fished waters, and there is a certain code that properly applies where many anglers gather on a popular pool or riffle. The casters should start toward the head of the water and work through in turn, each angler following the next and a decent interval behind. Thus each has an opportunity to test his skill the entire length of the pool, and no man may appropriate any one spot as his own without soon learning by hint, or plain forcible language, that he is not playing the game.

But let a fish be hooked and start his unpredictable speedy run, and all lines in range will at once come from the water, or should, and the lucky angler will be tendered advice as well as real assistance if needed in landing his fish.

Most anglers will respect legally closed waters, which are restricted by the authorities for conservation reasons, but privately posted areas will often provoke them to wrath. Here is presented a problem of increasing significance with respect to our future privileges of hunting and fishing. Trespass laws are usually definite and strict to protect the landowner, and rightly so. Too often the farmer has suffered seriously from the carelessness and depredations of unprincipled so-called sportsmen. A gate left open may mean the loss of valuable livestock. Hunters shoot domestic animals and barnyard fowl and even pepper the owner's dwelling.

It is the unthinking careless sportsman, and the utter vandal, who have put the landowner up in arms against all sportsmen as a class. Thus the burden is upon every right-minded outdoors lover to try to promote a better understanding. Very often the proper approach and request to fish or hunt with due regard for the farmer's rights and property will result in an invitation to do so, and so promote a mutual feeling of respect that augurs well for the future when more and more public lands will be under private control.

The angler should by all means support any serious conservation group in his locality, and not merely by paying dues and voting "aye" at the meetings. He should take an active part and voice his views clearly upon important matters with which he is conversant, not with immediate personal interest in mind but with the thought of helping to preserve for posterity the already dwindling steelhead run.

The individual's behavior and personal ethics play an important part regardless of regulations, for there is no control of the angler's actions when he is alone, perhaps far up in one of the great river canyons. He has only his conscience to guide him. In the foregoing discussion, I have dealt with various phases of the angler's attitude toward fishing as the principal desire which takes him afield. But actually most of us find much more that is good on the broad swift river of which we have dreamed through the long off-season. We go to enjoy the beauty and charm of the green forest-cloaked mountains, to sense the tang of wood smoke in the keen clean air of early morning, the fog-shrouded mystery of a wide tidal lagoon at daybreak, the restless energy of the great Pacific as its rollers break in endless succession upon the river bar.

We enjoy the wild flowers in their fern-bordered nooks among the rocks and watch for wild game. We stop on the river bar to study the multitudinous tracks of the wild things that claimed this narrow highway for their own last night. A winging flock of mallards high in the fading sunset of an October day brings us pause and contemplation and new appreciation of all the wonders of the great outdoors. The rustle of the alder and willow leaves in the warm breeze of evening is a soft requiem to our attuned ears.

And always there is the diapason of the mighty river, now swelling to a roar of bass notes on the riffle and dying to the low, sweet, minor tones as the water folds smoothly into the dark pool below. Sure, there are great silvery steelhead waiting there, but again I think of that old truism, whose author I do not know, and say most devoutly, "It is not all of fishing to fish!"

JIM TEENY
Gresham, Oregon

Born in Portland, Oregon, in 1945, Jim Teeny began fly fishing when he was twelve. In 1962, he originated the famous Teeny Nymph Fly. In 1971, he started the Teeny Nymph Company, and he currently designs and markets T-Series Fly Lines.

Teeny has appeared widely on television and video. His series, *Fly Fishing With Jim Teeny*, ran for six years in Tacoma, Washington, and he has made guest appearances on *Fly Fishing the West*, with Larry Schoenborn, and *The Fishing Hole*, with Jerry McKinnis. His instructional videos include *Basic Nymph Fishing*, *Fly Fishing Still Waters*, *Russian Rainbows*, *Fly Fishing for Salmon*, and the award-winning *Catching More Steelhead*. Teeny also travels on the show lecture circuit.

He is the author of *The Teeny Technique for Steelhead and Salmon*.

Memories of Bad Etiquette

*M*any years ago, while I was in high school, but still too young to drive, my dad would take me fishing. We went mostly for steelhead and occasionally some salmon. A friend and classmate of mine also liked to fish for steelhead and claimed to be quite successful. For some reason, he never invited me to go on his fishing trips, but he always wanted to go with my dad and me. Every once in a while I would ask my dad if we could take him along, and he would always say no.

This friend of mine was always bragging about the fish he caught, but would never tell me where he fished. This procedure went on for quite some time, him begging to be taken to our favorite spot on the river, and my dad holding out and refusing to do it. Finally, for whatever reason, my dad gave in and agreed to let my buddy accompany us. Of course, my friend was quick to say yes to coming along.

Early that next morning the three of us headed out for one of our special, secret spots, on one of our great rivers. As was usually the case, the fishing was quite good that day. We all caught a lot of steelhead and had a wonderful day together.

The next weekend rolled around, and I asked my dad if we

could again bring my friend along. This time my dad agreed again. I called his house to invite him, and to my disappointment, he was unable to go, but thanked me for inviting him. We chatted for awhile, and during the course of our conversation I must have mentioned the time that we were leaving the next morning.

We got an early start, stopping for breakfast along the way. When we pulled into our parking spot, I was very surprised to see my friend's car there. Then it occurred to me that his plans must have changed at the last minute, and he was going to be able to join us after all.

However, this thought soon changed. There he was with his younger brother, complete with a lantern. It turned out he wanted to be the first one at our special spot, our secret hole.

I felt just awful, because I had literally begged my dad, time and time again, to let this "friend" come along with us to fish. I had promised my father that my friend would respect and honor the fact that we were sharing one of our best fishing spots with him.

I learned that lesson the hard way, and it is one that I have never forgotten, the lesson about sharing, or not sharing, your secret spots.

Another fishing trip that I will always look back on was a trip to Oregon's East Lake in the fall of the year. In fact, this is the lake where I first originated the Teeny Nymph pattern.

There was a group of five or six of us, and we had planned a trip to go after large Eastern brook trout and German browns. We were there sometime in October, and the lake always closes at the end of the month. During this time of year the weather there is very unpredictable. It tends to get cold and nasty very quickly. At an elevation of 6,200 feet, the possibility of snow is quite good, and we thought we might encounter some on that particular day. Fortunately, the weather held out and the temperature was very comfortable.

As I recall, we were fishing on the north shore of this 2,200-acre lake. And at that time of year, we were not too surprised to have the whole lake to ourselves. The fishing from the shore was excellent, as both the browns and brookies were holding very close to the banks.

As we were enjoying the success of our fishing and the beauty and serenity of the day, we noticed a boat way off in the distance. It came closer and closer and closer, and then it simply trolled right over our lines! We were all shocked, and a couple of my buddies thought that we should go after them and punch them out. That didn't happen, but words were exchanged, making for an unpleasant day for all concerned.

What that man did that day was totally unsportsmanlike, and should never be a part of fishing. I will never forget him or the unpleasant and unnecessary experience.

Steelhead fishing today is much more difficult than in past years. When our runs were strong it was much easier on everyone. Now, especially in the West Coast area, we have fewer numbers of fish. Our license sales are down with the lack of fish. Fortunately, the fishermen we now run into seem to be of high quality, respecting both our fishery and the resource.

Steelhead fishing in Oregon, Washington, and California is down in numbers. But, it's not all doom and gloom, as some rivers have good strong numbers of fish. Action in a positive manner is being taken to help restore our once-wonderful runs.

———⟨∞⟩———

MICHAEL BAUGHMAN
Ashland, Oregon

His great-grandfather, John Brant, descendant of
Mohawk Chief Joseph Brant, taught Michael to fish on
a Pennsylvania trout stream when he was five. A few
years later his family moved to Hawaii, where he speared
fish through his reckless teenage years. He and his wife,
Hilde, have been fly fishing in Oregon rivers for four
decades. His articles, essays, stories, and poems have
appeared in many national magazines, including
National Wildlife and *Gray's Sporting Journal.* For several
years he was a special contributor to *Sports Illustrated,*
where most of his work dealt with the outdoors and the
environment.

His books include *Mohawk Blood, A River Seen Right,*
and *Warm Springs Millennium.*

The Gentleman at Fairview
From *A River Seen Right—A Fly Fisherman's North Umpqua,*
Lyons and Burford, 1995

We all know that humans mature as they grow older, and not
just physically; we also know that different individuals reach
remarkably different levels of maturity. These same observations can be applied in obvious ways to fishermen: Serious
anglers are apt to go through a number of identifiable stages in
their development, and this is particularly true of fly fishermen,

simply because, as a group, they are the most dedicated and passionate anglers of all.

Most often, in the beginning, we want to catch a lot of fish; then big fish; then difficult fish, or rare fish, or different kinds of fish than we have caught before, or more of the same kinds of fish we have caught before but in different places. Even today, despite all the compelling arguments against it, many beginning fishermen are determined to kill what they catch to show it to someone to prove that they have been somewhere and done something. But if they stay with it for long, and particularly if they fish with flies, they begin to release some fish, or most fish, or all but trophy fish, or all but hatchery fish, or everything.

If we can call all of this a process of maturity, then the most mature angler I have ever met was an elderly gentleman I ran into at Fairview eighteen or twenty years ago. Watching from the bank I saw him raise and miss two nice fish in the upper end of the pool. Then, when I talked to him after he had finished, he explained that missing the fish was no disappointment. He had clipped all the points off of his flies and was happy to fish only for strikes.

"Why did you decide to do that?" I asked him. "Because you don't want to hurt the fish?"

"No, not that," he answered. "I've read a lot of Thoreau." He looked at me and I nodded to him, to indicate that I'd read Thoreau too, and then he went on. "I think it was in Walden where he wrote that a lot of men fish all their lives without ever realizing that fish isn't really what they are after. Well, a while back, I figured out that he was right, at least in my case. The fish are just a reasonable excuse to be out there. If I worry about them too much, I miss a lot of everything else, of what I'm really here for." The old man smiled happily. "Does that make any sense?"

"Sure," I said. "I remember that passage. I know what you mean."

But I was fairly young, then, and I didn't really quite believe in what he was trying to tell me. In fact, as soon as he'd left, I climbed down the bank to fish for the two steelhead he'd raised and was very happy to hook and land one of them.

Now, years later and no longer young, I still enjoy hooking and landing fish; but I also think I finally know what the old man meant, and I appreciate it—and (I hope I can explain this) the appreciation seems to be retroactive.

Fifteen years ago—even ten—if asked about my most vivid memories of the North Umpqua, I would immediately have thought of the biggest or wildest fish I'd ever hooked, or of those very rare days (two maybe three in a decade) when aggressive steelhead could be found in virtually every riffle and pool.

I still remember certain fish and certain days, and it makes me happy to know I'll always have those memories; but when I think back now over the years many other things are apt to come to mind.

On the trail side of the upper river, at a fairly remote place I know, a sleek river otter and the two small pups she was herding ahead of her slid over the lip of a waterfall with power and grace more effortless than any I've ever seen on a basketball court or athletic field.

As I sat on a warm streamside rock near Discovery, waiting for the sun to slide a little farther down in the sky, a fifty-pound beaver swam by me not five feet away, heading upstream toward the Log Pool. Without thinking about it, I said, "hello." He turned his head to stare at me, an inquisitive look in his bright brown eyes, dense dark fur beaded with water. He stared at me for at least a minute, swimming just hard enough in the current to hold his own. "You might as well go on," I finally told him, and he did, swimming upstream as unconcerned as he had been before we spoke.

About half way up the trail from Wright Creek to Rattlesnake, on a dark early morning, I thought I saw another fisherman, a surprisingly short, fat man, walking toward me down the trail. I had my mouth open to say hello when I suddenly realized it wasn't a fisherman, it was a bear. Just as I stopped walking, he did. Then he stood on his hind legs, wheeled around smoothly, dropped down to all fours, and lumbered back upstream. I went back toward Wright Creek, as wide awake as I've ever been at that hour.

(Frank Moore's nephew had a somewhat more exciting encounter at the Log Pool not long ago. He was wading deep, as you need to do there, when he heard something splashing in the shallow water behind him. When he turned, he saw a frolicking cougar, and when he yelled—a combination of surprise and fright—the big, wet cat trotted up the steep trail to the road and disappeared.)

There are deer and elk along the river, osprey and water ouzels, quail and grouse. In fall, on the best days after the maples have turned, when the big bronze Chinook are spawning on the shallow gravel bars, simply watching the river can give more pleasure then fishing it.

A long time ago, there was a rare winter day with two or three inches of fresh powder snow along the riverbanks, and with the cold blue-green water free of algae, and thus clearer and lovelier than in summer. As I waded into a pool above Copeland Creek a flock of whistling swans flew overhead in an elongated V, their stretched necks as long as their bodies, their wing spans six or seven feet, black bills and white undersides in sharp detail against a cold gray sky, so close that I heard the rushing hiss of their slow, powerful wing beats as they passed. I don't remember if I caught a fish on that day, but those swans will always be with me.

SETH NORMAN
Bellingham, Washington

Norman's reporting on police corruption led to a Pulitzer Prize nomination, the Jane Harrah Memorial Award, and a Golden Medallion for Print Media. He is associate editor and "Master of Meander" for *California Fly Fisher*, books editor for *Fly Rod & Reel*, and the author of *Meanderings of a Fly Fisherman, Flyfisher's Guide to Northern California,* and *A Fly Fisher's Guide to Crimes of Passion.*

Seth's essays, humor, and fiction have appeared in *The Christian Science Monitor, Gray's Sporting Journal, Outdoor Life,* and *Field & Stream,* as well as in most of the national fly-fishing magazines. He received the Robert Traver Award from the John Voelker Foundation and the Roderick Haig-Brown Award for a body of work representing the ethics of fly fishing.

Fish Tale Protocol and Other Expectations

*S*teelhead fishing—party bank angling, the last time I tried it. Angling en masse. A sport in which you must be simultaneously player and spectator. Crammed in, besieged and intruded upon, you cast for one of the Few Remaining—remnants of a gallant species doomed by Lumber and Agribiz, and by the politicians these businesses keep as pets. I don't like the crowds or the protocol of "combat." Hey, I live in Oakland.

"The best thing about steelheading is the stories," says Sky Parsons across his vise. "All the great stories."

Monday is tying night at Sky's. About to take off to the Florida Keys, he's wrapped another Crazy Charley and now hesitates between brown and green calf tails. "Not just stories—great stories. Did I tell you about the time I got up so early, waded out when it was dark for these fish I'd spotted the evening before? So I'm waiting for the sun, positively gleeful that I have this pod all to myself . . . and I hear this splashing . . . splashing, which turns out to be Bill Shaadt coming up behind me. I mean, the man must have smelled them. Anyway, he's such a nice guy, we talk for hours . . . ."

I love stories, I truly do. Sky's always good for a couple. Now disguised as an elementary school teacher, he's also been a smuggler in Africa, a Caribbean yacht mercenary, a ne'er-do-well in Polynesia. His tales soothe the tension I incur while weaving another sort-of-bitchy stonefly nymph, ugly and fishable, like everything else in my box. The ugly part, anyway.

"Did I ever tell you about when I got ciguatera in Bora Bora? Thought I would die. No—thought I would die and was afraid I might not . . . ."

I miss North Carolina mainly for the stories: southerners still talk the talk. For the sake of stories I read—daily, nightly—as if paid by the word. Since I love fishing, adding fishing and words together should be a treat. I can almost imagine the scene: Sloshing into the line-up with my eight-weight I work a shooting head out through the tip top, turn to six fishers on my left then the nine on my right and, delicately, suggest that I'm ready for True Life Tales. By way of encouragement—give a story to get one—I begin my own: "So there I am in the Sea of Galilee, circa 1971, Saint Peters fish rising all around me—a thousand puckering mouths. Then the Mirages streak over, three of them, roaring toward the Golan . . . well that put the fish right down. But wait, I know that heavy percussion will trigger a midge hatch in ten or twenty minutes . . . ."

Yep, I could enjoy that. Or I would, I suppose, if that's what I expected. There's the rub against the grain.

Example: I went party boat fishing often during my misspent youth, cheek to jowl with anchovies and the unwashed, elbowing my way to the stern in my turn. I caught fish, pocketed a jackpot once in a luckily while, and drove home happy, flush with a sense of "Got what I came for."

The satisfaction's similar, however different the experience, to that of hiking out from a remote trickle with a memory brimming of brook trout. What I came for, hoped to find, needed. My problem is that when I seek rivers, part of what I want is solitude.

"I mean, with steelheading, the people are a big part of it," Sky continues. "Talking, maybe learning something, or just laughing to keep warm."

I can see the pleasure when he frames it that way, contemplate a clubby casting klatch in the cold where folks compare flies and tactics, get a hook-up every other day. Sort of low stakes fish-poker in bad weather. Somebody offered a similar perspective last Thursday, though I didn't quite see it at the time. Brett Jensen guides the Klamath and other waters, but loves the Klamath best and has for decades. He's also a talented photographer, with pictures in "Angler's Calendar." Sometimes he does a slide for clubs: among the misty vistas and gray green moments he's captured, shots in which you feel the melding of forest and water and sky, there's suddenly this shot of a pram line, boats grappled together so close that you can smell the neighbor's coffee and hear the little cliques.

"Salmon line at Chetco Tide Rock," Jensen says brightly. I'd have rather seen a photo of worst-case reactions to ringworm. I mean, here I'm drifting a coastal river reverie and suddenly I'm confronted with a brigade of anglers who look a lot like my classmates at traffic school, only colder.

"Now I know how this looks," Jensen continues quickly, "and these guys can be clannish. But they're really a good bunch, and it's a lot of fun out there. Last year, somebody anchored way out in the middle ordered pizza, delivered, and we all passed it over. Next time . . . ." Next time . . . Eureka. Next time Brett will arrive knowing what to expect, without a loose hope in his head—no expectations of a quiet space, a lone osprey, a river whispering through the riffles. And if your fishing isn't equated with sly stalks and long walks, delicate presentations observed only by osprey—if you're from downtown Brooklyn or Bombay and love it there, or grew up so far out in the Gobi that seeing lots of people is a hoot—you could enjoy this get together.

Seriously. Play some music, bring the little woofers. Share sandwiches. Pass a bottle—"Believe I will." Brag on flies, rods, tactics. Catch a salmon or steelhead once in a while, watch other fishers catch them. Lie about last time. Make new friends or talk about friends no longer around. Ask advice or give it. Tell jokes; repeat them, embellish. Make up completely untrue tales, like "Did you know that the Johnson Nymph is saturated in Preparation H, no kidding—they say it's the shark oil?" Trade beers, arrange marriages, promote causes, sell life insurance and major appliances.

It could be fun. There's some fishing in there too, not necessarily lost amid other items on the agenda. To be sure, after a few such days you'd be less prone to get cranky about the mobbed parking lot at Hat Creek below Power House Two. Instead you'd gaze about you with a smile, acknowledging plenty of company, plenty of fish, satisfied to have enough space for a back cast. Certainly this attitude would make you a much happier camper than the person lashing his rod back and forth and swearing "Dammit! Ten years ago . . . ." (or twenty, or two).

Could this be the way of the future? Some time back I indulged a puzzled musing, trying to explain to myself why so many fly fishers seemed determined to fish so few locations. Too busy, I reasoned, no time to explore a world so wide and high. Many people prefer smooth spring creeks of which there are few; also, if it's lots of big fish an angler wants—who doesn't— that's delimiting. Still, it bothered me. I mean, any Saturday in

Feather River country there must be hundreds of miles of creeks tumbling down without wetting a felt-soled boot . . . .

So what?

Listening to Sky I realize that many fishers don't expect to be alone, to fish a run first that day, see only tracks of deer and raccoon. Isolation isn't, automatically, an ingredient required to make the day rise. Not only that—when I stop to think—in lots of places solitude hasn't been part of the game for centuries: on English chalk streams, private and expensive, where you're not allowed near the water unless a ghillie is along; on those Eastern rivers of legend with long, cool Indian names, where the opening day hordes look vast as any that ever came our of a steppe.

"And that's what it going to be like, for the rest of your fishing life," says the angry crank at Hat Creek or Hot, remembering, cursing. "Scads of people. Everywhere."

"Might as well be steelheading," I admit.

He glares. "But I like steelheading."

I glare back. He continues. "I know, I know. But did I tell you about the time—on the Smith, I think it was . . . ."

Could be I'll find him at Sky's house some Monday night, a place where I expect good conversation.

Part Six

FISHING FINE AND FAR OFF

A Glimpse into Customs Afar

As the world becomes smaller, travel becomes easier, and the popularity of the sport of angling continues to increase, many fishermen are traveling to foreign destinations to fish for new species, and seek new adventures. Consequently, this section might be of interest to those who either have already been, and to those who plan to go.

GLENN LAW
Princeton, New Jersey

Glenn Law is an award-winning writer who began his career as a guide on the Madison River. He was an outdoor columnist for the *Bozeman Daily Chronicle* and later, the *Miami Herald*. He is the former editor of *Florida Sportsman Magazine* and senior editor for *Salt Water Sportsman*. He has been writing and editing magazines and books for twenty years and is author of *A Concise History of Fly Fishing*.

The British Traditions
From *A Concise History of Fly Fishing*,
The Lyons Press, 2003

The British traditions were well established, and they were not without their own severe dogma. Many of the rules, especially of the hallowed Hampshire waters, were not even a consideration to the Americans. The British tradition, where we leave it, made specific demands upon the angler. Codes of conduct and expectations of behavior, concepts of propriety on the English chalk streams are quite foreign to the American tradition.

Consider: On the beats of the Hampshire streams, the anglers even today fish only to rising fish. Fishing the water is thought less than civilized. Getting in the water is deemed equally as boorish. Carefully manicured, the chalk streams are absolutely never waded; rather, rising fish are fished from the bank once they have been observed feeding on the surface. The dry fly is used preferentially—even today it is a more aristocratic approach—and only when that brings no result is the upstream nymph brought into play.

The British terminology "killing" a trout is not to be taken lightly. It is generally accepted that once a trout is caught, it's groceries. Return a trout to the river and it becomes a bottom-feeder. As such it'll never be caught again, because anglers on these streams never fish on the bottom.

Feeling a bit stifled, a bit constrained in your fishing? Let's pack our bags and cross the Atlantic where fly fishing gets a new start on fresh waters.

JOHN GODDARD
United Kingdom

John Goddard has fished lakes and streams worldwide, but he knows the chalk streams of Southern England intimately. In recent years, he has also taken many species of saltwater fish on fly, including large bonefish, permit, and sailfish.

He is the author of nine books, and he is a regular contributor to fly fishing periodicals both in the U.K. and abroad. Goddard is a skilled micro-photographer and an accomplished fly dresser, with many patterns to his credit.

Fishing Manners in the United Kingdom
The Chalk Streams of Yorkshire, Southern, and South West England

I am fortunate to be living within easy reach of all the major chalk streams and other well known rivers of Southern England, and have been very privileged to have had the opportunity to fly fish most of these over the past forty years. During this period I have fished from time to time most of the famous beats on the River Test, and if one looks back over the history of fly fishing, particularly fishing the dry fly, it is a matter of record that much of the etiquette relating to this wonderful sport of ours was established on this king of dry fly waters.

There are, of course, many aspects of etiquette that the fly fisher should take into account—all of which are more than adequately covered in this book, so I do not intend to touch upon any of these. However, when it comes to some of the major aspects, if and when these are ignored by other fly fishers, it can completely upset the pleasure of a day's fishing. Particularly if one has had to remonstrate with the angler concerned.

During the course of my long angling career, I have found that most anglers, particularly fly fishers, are very tolerant, helpful, polite, and obey the general rules of etiquette. Unfortunately, as in every walk of life, there are exceptions.

The world famous chalk streams of England are fed by

aquifers [reservoirs] of water deep beneath the hills. This results in a flow of very pure, clear water with but little variation in temperature throughout the year. These streambeds, compiled of chalk and gravel, are highly alkaline and produce huge quantities of weeds which provide both sanctuary for the fish and also ideal breeding conditions for the many species of aquatic insects for which these streams are famous.

Unfortunately, most of these chalk streams, not unlike other rivers worldwide, are now suffering from both water abstraction and chemical pollution. Pesticides and herbicides leach into these streams from the agricultural land bordering them. It is very sad to relate that due to this run-off, the huge hatches of insects that used to occur on these streams are now but a shadow of what they used to be.

Fishing on these chalk streams is very exclusive and expensive. Without exception, they are all privately owned. They are divided into "beats," usually a half-mile long, and let [rented] to rods on a seasonal basis, usually for one, or in some cases two, set days per week.

Today, if you want to fish on one of these streams it will mean obtaining a personal introduction to one of the landowners—and then, if you are lucky—you may be offered a place on a waiting list, which means in four or five years time you may be offered a rod! A rod on one of the better known chalk streams such as the Test or the Itchen can be very expensive and are generally rented for one day a week for the season. Sometimes tackle shops are able to offer day tickets to fish a beat on selected stretches at a cost of around 150 pounds per day. Even today, the trout fishing on these streams can be excellent, with both brown and, in some cases, rainbow trout averaging two to three pounds. Although it must be realized that while there are still some wild fish in these streams, most of the larger fish will have been stocked.

Should you be fortunate enough to have the opportunity to fish one of these streams, you will be expected to observe strict rules and etiquette that have been established over the centuries. Only one fly is allowed, and this must be fished and cast only upstream. Most landowners allow you two brace of trout, and after these have been caught, fishing must cease. Fishing the water [blind fishing] is frowned upon as you are expected to cast only to either rising trout, or when nymph fishing, only to the trout you can see. On most chalk streams you are not allowed to fish a nymph until after the first of July, and wading, except under unusual circumstances, is not encouraged. If you are fishing a beat where there are other rods fishing too, you should never walk downstream close to the bank. Furthermore, when passing another fly fisher who may be fishing or observing, you should always give him a wide berth and ask permission to fish above him.

Guides in the U.K.

Guides are rarely to be found in the U.K., and in most cases, are not really necessary. However, on some of the big trout lakes and reservoirs where you fish from boats, they are available, but are usually referred to as gillies, not guides. On many salmon beats in Scotland gillies are obligatory.

Catch and Release

I was probably one of the first writers, over twenty years ago, to try and influence British fly fishers to adopt no-kill fisheries. In those early days that was very hard work, but gradually more and more landowners, of both moving and still water, are allowing catch and release. Opinions vary widely, however, with a hardcore of nearly fifty percent of our fly fishers still against the practice. However, I am still strongly in favour, particularly on those small streams in Scotland, Ireland, Wales, and the West Country that are not stocked, and rely on their indigenous populations of wild brown trout. The newly formed Wild Trout Society already has membership of over 100,000 fly fishers, and it is now strongly in favour of catch and release, in an effort to preserve the fishing for our grandchildren. I am also delighted to note that, at long last, some of our authorities governing salmon fishing here are now talking of restricting individual catches and encouraging release.

My Pet Hates:

1. You are kneeling down casting to a rising fish when another angler strolls up behind you to pass the time of day, consequently spooking the fish to which you are casting.

2. You may be standing observing the water, or even casting to a fish, when another angler appears walking along the bank. Upon seeing you he should pass, giving you a wide berth and keeping well away from the water for at least a hundred yards. This angler has either never heard of this rule or is very selfish, as he pushes past you and proceeds to walk above you, as close to the river as possible, spooking every fish in a large area.

3. Almost as bad is the fly fisher fishing along the bank on the opposite side of the river who behaves in the same way. The above three instances of course apply particularly when fishing on chalk streams or spring creeks, which are rarely very wide.

4. You are salmon or steelhead fishing a pool, working your way up it, when another fly fisher pushes in front and commences fishing there, instead of following along at a reasonable distance behind you.

5. When fly fishing from a boat on a big lake or reservoir and drift fishing, other boats should not pass in front of you for at least a couple of hundred yards. Of all the rules of etiquette, this is the one that is ignored more than any other. In fact, I am sure that many fly fishers are completely unaware of it. On the other hand, common sense must surely apply here—if fly fishers are fishing downwind from a boat drifting with the wind, if you pass over their line of drift, you will surely scare away any fish in that vicinity.

6. In the U.K., when fly fishing on still water from a boat, you will rarely see the really accomplished fly fisher standing up to cast. With a little practice you can learn to cast almost as far sitting down as when standing. Despite this, you will often observe quite a large proportion of boat anglers standing up to cast. All this achieves is to drive the fish further away from the boat, as the higher you are above the surface of the water, the further away the fish can see you.

   Apart from this, yet another factor must be taken into account, at least in a flat calm. Under these conditions any ripple emanating from the boat is likely to scare away any fish in the near vicinity. And when standing up to cast, particularly when trying to cast any distance, the arm motion this far above the center of gravity of the boat will rock it quite violently, sending out more of a wave than a ripple.

7. While on the subject of boat fishing, why is it that so many fly fishers seem to wear bright clothing in this medium, which can only help to alert the fish to their presence? In

most cases, these same anglers, when fishing from a bank of a river or stream would probably wear either camouflaged or subdued clothing.

8. Finally, I should like to raise a point where rules of etiquette do not apply, where it is more a question of common sense. If you are a keen stillwater fly fisher, you will surely have found yourself in this situation on many occasions:

You have arrived early at the waterside and are fishing from the bank. The water is fairly shallow and though you could enter and wade out to where it is deeper, you decide (quite rightly) that any trout in the vicinity are just as likely to come into the shallows to feed, particularly if you stay out of the water and keep all movement to a minimum. Unfortunately for you, the average fly fisher rarely considers this, as most of them have one thought in mind which is to cast out as far as possible into the water to increase the distance. They will immediately wade out. The only thing this achieves is, again, to drive the fish further out. It also means that the early arrival who was fishing quietly from the bank has no option (other than moving to another location) but to wade out and join them.

Rudy van Duijnhoven
Groesbeek, Holland

Rudy van Duijnhoven is a freelance photographer and author. He has published his work in several countries, including the United States, where he travels and fishes often. He is also the European correspondent for *Fly Fishing in Salt Waters*.

Rudy has won the Best of the West Casting Competition in San Mateo, California, where he stopped people in their tracks to watch his beautiful, effortless casting style.

The Flatlands—The Netherlands
Proper Behavior

1. Do not do to someone else, what you would not like him to do to you; wise words that apply to a lot of the ethics considered normal in fishing.

2. Keep your distance to other fishermen, not only when you are actually fishing, but also when you pass them on your way to another spot.

3. The bottom, especially in the many polders, is very soft and easily passes on vibrations. Wakes of fish spreading in all directions is the outcome of walking too close to the water. And a scared fish is of course very difficult to catch.

4. When you walk into a meadow, always close the gates behind you. If farmers have to catch escaped cattle because you left a gate open, they will not be too pleased with your presence. It could well mean the loss of fishing rights for the club, so think before you act.

5. High grass that has been trampled upon cannot be cut and harvested anymore, so stay out of meadows with long grass.

6. Carp fishermen hiding behind some weeds while trying to keep out of sight will not be amused when you show up next to them standing upright like a lighthouse along a beach.

7. Do not leave any trash behind, but deposit it in a waste bag along the road or at the place where you are staying.

8. Nylon especially can be a bird killer, and baited hooks or flies hanging from a branch or cable will be taken by birds and bats.

9. Only fish in those waters that you are allowed to fish according to the licenses you have bought. Although the penalties for fishing in waters without the necessary licenses are still relatively mild compared with other countries, it is just not done.

10. Most Dutch anglers only "keep" their catch these days on slides or color negative film. So return any fish to the water again as soon as possible.

11. Only keep one or two fish that you might want to eat that same day. Fish that you want to keep are killed first before you attempt to remove the hook.

12. People fishing a certain area from one side of a boat should be passed on the opposite side. No one would like it when a hot spot is spoiled by a boat passing at short distance, so keep an open eye for these circumstances. Especially when you make use of an outboard engine, you should keep your distance to other boats. Fish like sea bass are easily put down by the noise of such an engine.

13. Stay out of the fairway when looking for a place to anchor. This is extremely dangerous, especially when the visibility is poor, due to fog for instance.

14. Be careful with the equipment you hire (boat, fishing rods) and return them in the state you received them. Tell when something has broken or has been lost.

15. When you are having good success with a certain fly and fishing method, share these with your fellow fishermen. Give them the same fly and show them how to fish it. You will appreciate that you did this when things are not working for you on another day and your friends help you out at that moment.

Surprisingly, being a country where some 14 million people live on a surface of around 200 by 250 kilometers, The Netherlands still have a lot to offer to the angler. Although growing in popularity, I would estimate that only ten- to fifteen thousand of these people use a fly rod on most of their outings.

KEITH POND
New Brunswick, Canada

Keith Pond grew up on the Miramichi River and is currently the fourth generation owner/operator of the historic salmon lodge now known as Pond's Resort. After obtaining a degree in forestry, Keith returned to the river, where he has spent his life in pursuit of Atlantic salmon. He has seen tremendous changes in the past forty years, both in the fishery and the fishermen. The following is written from the point of view of both an angler and a lodge owner, providing an unusual perspective on a distinctive aspect of fly fishing, and the etiquette that accompanies it.

Eastern Canada
Changing Customs in the Camps

Years ago the traditional fly-fisher guest that came to the Miramichi was an older, gruffer type of gentleman. There were very few female fishing guests, and those that came only came with their husbands. In the past few years the age of our guests has dropped noticeably. They seem to be more refined, better educated, less rigid in their thoughts, and there are a lot more women participating in salmon fishing today.

In the bar one evening before supper I introduced a lady guest to a couple of older (and definitely "old school") gents who were staying in camp as well. One guy said to her, "You cast pretty good—for a woman." And she replied, without batting an eye, "You cast pretty good for an asshole."

Afterward, the lady was horrified that she had said this— said it just came out of her mouth before she had a chance to think. The fellow took it extremely well, and gave her credit for a quick retort. Times have certainly changed, and with them, the camp etiquette.

It is customary to rotate through fishing pools on the Miramichi. We have a regular guest who is a fanatical fisherman, and very precise in everything he does. He is quite exacting about pool etiquette as well. He was fishing our home pool with other guests, and was not happy with the angler who was down river from him in the good pool. This guy did not seem to be moving through the pool at a rate that was acceptable, so our regular guest called down to him and asked, "Is your ass glued to a rock, right there in that spot?" Yes, times *have* changed.

With respect to tipping, it is customary to tip the guides between 15 percent to 25 percent per guide/per day (Canadian) depending, of course, on how happy you are with the level of service. For the lodge staff the norm is $50 per guest per three-day stay (2004 rates). And incidentally, no non-resident may fish for *any* species without being accompanied by a licensed guide in this province.

In Eastern Canada it is mandatory for non-residents to purchase a three-day, seven-day, or seasonal license. Regulations differ greatly between provinces and river systems such as the Miramichi, the Restigouche, and the Grand Cascapedia. A foreigner cannot fish without a guide on the Miramichi. This river has lots of lodges with private water. The Grand Cascapedia has its own special system: an arrangement between the landowners and the government was established, whereby all the private lodges open a section of their waters (pools which are rotated) to the public who are afforded the opportunity to fish there, by way of an annual lottery system. If an angler lands, or even hooks, any species, their fishing is over for that day, the rule being one fish hooked per day per angler. The Restigouche is mostly closed, corporately owned, with private camps offering very little opportunity for the public to access it.

We have seen a noticeable difference in the fishing since the inception of catch and release. Yes, our catch-and-release program began in 1983, and it took about four years before we started seeing great results. The results have grown yearly since then, and in the early '90s, when the last of the commercial salmon nets were removed from the east coast salt waters, the increase in fish population was phenomenal. Almost instantaneous! And, it brought back the large fish (the 30- to 40-pounders) that we hadn't seen in the river in years. Our river used to be known for its higher percentage of grilse, compared to mature salmon, but now that has reversed.

We are proud of our fishery and of our beautiful waters here in New Brunswick. Anglers like our hook-and-release rules, and the Miramichi still has the largest runs of Atlantic salmon on the east coast of North America and Great Britain.

Hopefully, with good management and support this trend will continue into the future.

JIM REPINE
Futaleufu, Chile

Jim Repine and his wife, Sonia, operate a trout fly fishing lodge in the southern part of Chile, high in the Andes.

Jim is the author of several books, including *Pacific Rim Fly Fishing: The Unrepentant Predator*. His angling and business experiences have taken him around the Pacific Rim, where he has enjoyed experiencing trout in many different beautiful and unusual settings.

Chile

$\mathscr{F}$ly fishing has been practiced for a long time in Chile, but only by a rare few. Now, it's not unlike Japan when I lived there in the '50s. In similar fashion, until recently in Chile (within the last ten years or so) there weren't enough anglers here for ethics to matter. In that decade, and after several hundred days on Chilean water, 95 percent of the time, even now, *when* and *where* I fish, no one else is around. Bear in mind, I tend to seek that ambiance. Time on a trout stream with solitude (except for my dog) is my spiritual penicillin.

But, things are beginning to change. A narrow escape from communism in 1973, followed with a dictator who believed in free market economics, resulted in a long period of general prosperity. It's still growing, and the best economy in South America has resulted in a rapidly expanding middle class (shades of post-war Japan), with more and more money and time. The global spread of traveling anglers and a mini-boom in local interest is beginning to make an impact. Good news or bad?

The economic value of visiting fishers to small rural communities on or close to good fishing can be helpful, as long as there are good regulations and strong enforcement. Sadly, Chile has neither. In neighboring Argentina, after a total of less than fifty days of fishing over the same years, I have been checked for a license three times. Here it has never happened to me or anyone else I know of.

I fish mostly in southern Chile, between Temuco and Puerto Mont, in the 200-mile stretch known as the Lake District, that Haig-Brown wrote most about. Remarkable then as now, this is a region of world-class scenery and lots of gorgeous lakes, rivers, and streams. Tragically, the fishery has been so debauched since Brown was there, that it is of little or no interest to anglers anymore. The point is, even at the polar caps there is no "alone" these days. How arrogant we are to think so!

"O, the gallant fisher's life,
It is the best of any;
And't is beloved by many."
—Izaak Walton, 1653

In the south, at first urgent need of regulation enforcement didn't seem pressing, given the few fishermen seen. There were lots of fish and fair numbers of large fish, but only because of light pressure. Having watched Alaska's fishery for twenty years, I know what pressure can do and how quickly. The natural preservative of difficult access will only slow the depletion of these fish as it has in Alaska, but the potential for irreparable harm is even greater here. It is a very fragile fishery. It has neither the rich bug life of Montana nor the massive salmon runs of Alaska. With few exceptions, trophy trout here are old trout. The Chilean Government is environmentally asleep, and most Chileans, in lamentable ignorance, kill every fish they catch. If I hadn't been so intrigued with the capture of wild creatures, I may never have discovered the higher joy of freeing them. The most needed ethic in southern Chile is as simple as it is obvious. Stop killing fish—now—before the results of mindless destruction are irreversible.

Happily, Chile is Chile. Needful of no comparisons, this superb compilation of geography still offers excellent populations of *truchas grandes* [large trout]—rainbows, brookies and browns. It is a blessed land, gorgeous from snow-capped mountains, across lush fertile valleys, to a lovely seacoast extending from close to the Equator south for three thousand miles. The farther south one goes, the less exploited fishing will be. Tierra del Fuego, though barren and wind swept, is the unquestioned, least "hit on" fish-filled wilderness left on the planet. Fly fishing lodges (my wife owns one) are more numerous every season yet as of now, offer no threat.

As the unrestricted do-it-yourselfers from home and abroad increase, the threat magnifies. Unless you come here not only as a strong conservationist, but also as the bearer of the conservationist word, understand that you will only be contributing to the destruction of one of the last superb angling areas left on the planet. There are moves afoot, proposals and so forth (I have one), though nothing needful of bureaucratic support moves quickly in Chile. The great race is for regs and fish cops to arrive in time to stave off the final onslaught of the bad guys. If that happens in time, we can then turn our attention to things like how long each angler should work a pool before giving it up to the next gal or guy. Will we make it? It's scary, but I haven't lost hope yet.

MARCOS CZERWINSKI
Río Grande, Argentina

After retiring from the Argentine Air Force in 1985, Czerwinski settled down in Bahía Blanca, Buenos Aires province, where he opened Angler's Aventuras Fly Shop in 1986. After introducing fly fishing to many and planting the seeds of a fly fishing association there, he moved the fly shop and his family (wife and three boys) to Río Grande in Tierra del Fuego, in 1990.

For many years he ran a fishing operation at the

Estancia María Behety, on the Río Grande in Tierra del Fuego. Now he runs his own lodge, on the same river, but in Chile. He is the IGFA representative for Argentina.

Fly Fishing Etiquette and Customs in Argentina

*I*t was not until the 1950s that the good fishing in remote places (not so remote nowadays) was "discovered" by a few Argentine anglers who went fishing there, bringing home many big trout along with pictures. Later, after some of their fishing friends from Europe and North America saw the pictures and tasted the fish, the word spread all over the small international fishing community, which was already turning from the bait and artificial lures toward fly fishing.

Between the '50s and '70s, the small Argentine fly fishing community began to achieve the fishing techniques and polite manners of the sport and transferred them to the very few newcomers of the considered "snobbish sport" of those days.

In the '70s, fly fishing started to be increasingly popular, with many more fishermen on the rivers and lakes. But nobody was teaching manners at all. The important teaching came later. First there were some very elementary lessons about fishing techniques from a few fly-fishing associations. Later—thanks to the media—came a strong message regarding good fishing etiquette, focusing mainly on the catch-and-release method, which, in many ways, includes good and polite manners.

In the meantime, while the industry and the clubs were trying to educate the fast-growing fishing public in the north, tourism brochures were showing photos of huge dead trout hanging on fences by the numbers in the remote places in the south. This is the bad side of the story.

Beaching fish in scratchy nets leads to the death of many fish.

The good side of the story is that in most of those fishing regions in Patagonia and Tierra del Fuego, thanks to the educated fishermen, local governments started to look after the resource better. Rivers that were almost lost to the sport were recovered or are finally now being protected after a lapse of nearly two decades. The rivers and lakes that are still unreachable to the general public due to difficult or private access, are in very good shape and are giving us outstanding fishing. An excellent example is the Río Grande in Tierra del Fuego, Argentina.

The Río Grande [big river], whose tributaries were "planted" with Atlantic salmon and rainbow and brown trout by Mr. John Goodall, is a short, straight river, some eighty kilometers long, flowing to the Atlantic Ocean from the mountains. It is a river that was very seldom fished between 1935 and the '70s because it's not close to public roads; the population of the province was very small in those years and the local fishing community was even smaller. For the international fishing community, it wasn't easy to come by air from Buenos Aires, three thousand kilometers away. Consequently, the Río Grande was only fished by friends of the owners or the administrators of the *estancias* [estates, ranches].

All of the *estancias* with frontage on the river are running fishing operations now, with people coming from all over the world to fish for trophy trout, the sea run browns. In general, the fishing etiquette among the anglers fishing within those operations is impeccable, foreigners and Argentines as well.

But some kilometers from town, there is a public access to a small section of the river where etiquette is forgotten or unknown. Flies, lures and bait are all used and many disgusting situations are often witnessed between the locals, Argentines from the mainland, and the foreigners that fish by themselves and not through some fishing operation.

During the last decade, fly fishing has become so popular in Argentina, that now many more species are also being pursued with flies, such as the strong, beautiful and combative dorado *(Salminus maxillosus)*, as well as many minor species that were overlooked twenty years ago. The fishing population has increased tremendously, and lots of fly fishing associations have been founded. All of them are working hard, publishing information and advising national and provincial governments to help the public understand the manners of this sport that it so important as an economic and recreational activity. In some places, like in Tierra del Fuego's Río Grande city, fly fishing is being taught in some public and private schools too.

Very sadly, many good rivers are fished out nowadays, and no longer available to the general fishing community. But, we are looking forward with hope to see the results of our investment in education in fishing conservation and etiquette that the clubs, associations and foundations are making in Argentina.

These investments will surely pay off in the very short term if they are directed mostly to our children. Theirs are the rivers, streams and lakes along with all the fish that we can leave both to them and future generations for their enjoyment and profit.

JOSÉ RICARDO MATEU
Valencia, Spain

Mateu was born in 1965 and has traveled all of Spain to fly fish for trout. He's also fished the United States, Finland, Switzerland, Austria, Slovenia, and France. Not long ago, he translated and adapted into Spanish *Fly Casting Techniques* by Joan S. Wulff and *The Essence of Flycasting* by Mel Krieger. He teaches fly casting (certified by the FFF) at his school in Valencia.

Fly Fishing in Spain

Spain is seeing more and more fly fishers nowadays and you can even find some guide service in the better fly fishing areas. Like every place, there are certain areas in Spain which prevail over others for fly fishing (particularly for dry fly fishing) because they've always fly fished there, and therefore there is a great tradition. Besides, they have miles of world-class water, and the quality and variety of rivers is really incredible.

Proper Behavior and a Piece of Advice

There are some circumstances you have to be aware of when you come to Spain to fish. These are as follows:

1. First of all, obtain your respective license in the specific *autonomía* [state] you intend to fish. If you want to fish any of the stretches that we call *cotos* [ticket waters], get your permit within that province or contact the corresponding fishing club or guide service.

2. If the riverkeeper or gamekeeper asks for your license and/or permit, show it to him and be polite.

3. Crowds are not a problem at all (except for salmon and sea run brown trout fishing in the free waters of the north of Spain). Anyway, if you find someone fishing the same stretch of the river pass him by far enough from the riverbank, and remember to leave at least two or three hundred yards between him and yourself.

4. If a fly fisher is waiting for a dawn hatch in a certain spot or pool, move into another pool if you want to fish the same hatch. Spanish anglers will do the same when they see you in this situation. It's not usual that two fish the same pool at a time.

5. Generally, Spanish fly fishers are very kind. Many times they will share their experiences on the river and show you their flies, techniques, the best way to fish that spot, etc. I know you'll do the same.

6. What we call *pesca sin muerte* [catch and release] is quite widespread here among fly fishers, but not as much in salt water.

7. If you ever walk into a meadow, especially in the north of Spain, be careful with plants. Try walking alongside the meadows.

8. The major part of the land next to the rivers are public areas. However, if you ever hire a car, don't park on private property.

9. Be quiet when you fish for brown trout or native trout. They are very spooky, and generally the waters they inhabit are crystal clear.

10. Don't make any sort of fire or bonfire. Spain is a relatively dry country and the penalties are very strong.

11. Be aware of electric cables when walking into what we call *minicentrales hidroeléctricas* [little constructions similar to dams for making electricity].

12. When you fish in the north of Spain for Atlantic salmon, be aware of the quick changes in the level of the river waters: Some dams used to release reservoir waters with no warning at all. If you ever get there, talk to the fishers and inform yourself before you get into those big rivers. If you do so everything will be OK.

13. Some areas hold some cattle. They are not dangerous but you can prevent accidents if you just keep away from them.

Some rivers, like the Esla, the Porma, the Orbigo (some years ago considered the best in Europe for dry fly fishing), the Torío, the Duerna, and many more used to hold trout over twenty pounds. Here one fishes traditional flies, called "León wet flies," which are tied in a specific way. These antique patterns are unique to this area.

The Spanish native trout is the brown trout. In the north of Spain there are rivers where browns migrate to the sea and come back into the rivers to spawn. Unlike salmon they actually keep feeding. These anadromous brown trout are called *reo*. Conversely, we call the brown trout that stay permanently in freshwater *trucha común*.

There are also native Atlantic salmon *(Salmo salar)* in the north of Spain. Species like bigmouth bass, Danube salmon, rainbow trout, pike, carp, and *lucioperca*—a close relative of the walleye—were all introduced a long time ago into our rivers, and almost all of them have adapted extremely well. All of these species can be fished to with a fly rod.

Fly Fishing for Trout
You can choose to fish either in public water or in the *cotos* [ticket waters]. These areas were established sometime ago simply to control the fishing pressure in those places. Almost every one of the *cotos* are booked months in advance, so you must apply to fish these. This is a common tradition in Spain and we are used to it. Some of the *cotos* can be fished with a daily permit, which you can get on the spur of the moment, or some days in advance, at restaurants near the river. Nevertheless, most of our waters are public with free access. And some of them are even better than the ticket waters.

Fly Fishing for Atlantic Salmon
Not too many years ago, there used to be a lot of spawning runs of Atlantic salmon in our rivers, mainly in Asturias [in the north of Spain]. Unfortunately, this has changed due to several reasons (conservation, dam construction, etc.). Anyway, there's still a high possibility of catching an Atlantic salmon on a fly rod, as not many people try to catch them that way anymore.

Depending on the number of salmon entering the rivers, the best months would be May, June, July, and August. Rivers like the Narcea (I think this is the best), the Sella, the Eo, the Esva, and the Cares are all still good rivers. When the season opens there is an old tradition in Asturias regarding the first salmon caught in each one of the rivers. This first salmon is called *El Campanu* and some people pay quite a lot of money to eat this first Atlantic salmon. Some of the best pools to catch salmon on a fly rod are ticket waters and you have to ask for them nearly a year ahead of time.

If you get a *coto,* and the year has seen a good run of Atlantic salmon in the rivers, the possibilities of catching a salmon increase greatly.

There used to be huge salmon in these rivers but nowadays the average weight is between six and fourteen pounds. Despite these smaller weights, I assure you that it's still worth catching and fighting an Atlantic salmon with a single- or two-handed fly rod.

Nowadays, some conservation associations are fighting for the rivers in the north of Spain, trying to recover their magnificence of the past.

How to Get Your License

All the water in Spain is public so you can access and exit the river, or walk along the banks or in the river, with no problems.

Some years ago we had a unique national license with which we could fish the whole country. Ever since Spain was divided in several *autonomías,* each one of them them established its own fishing license. These days, you need a yearly license for each one of the *autonomías,* which cost about six or seven dollars apiece in 2004. Each *autonomía* is formed by several provinces. For example, Castellón, Valencia, and Alicante form the Comunidad Valenciana; and Teruel, Huesca, and Zaragoza together form Aragón. Each province has its own *consejería de medio ambiente* [Environmental Council] where you can get your license immediately. There are also some private companies (like banks) that can provide the licenses you need for the various *autonomías.*

Each province establishes its own *cotos* [ticket waters], so you must get a special permit from that province to fish there. These permits are even cheaper than the respective licenses. Each *coto* has its own regulations and customs. Once there, they will inform you about each one of the characteristics of the different ticket waters you have in that specific province. Some of them are stretches with introduced trout; others hold a wild or native population of trout.

There are also lots of fishing clubs which manage their own stretches of river and often offer a one-day permit. There are thousands of miles of free water in Spain, and some of it is very good for both dry and wet fly fishing.

JOHN KENT
Christchurch, New Zealand

Kent, a retired medical practitioner, was born and raised in Christchurch, but he has lived on both the North and

South Islands of New Zealand. He has held a New Zealand trout fishing license for the past forty-eight years, and has tramped and fished extensively throughout both islands, as well as fishing in Montana and Alaska.

He wrote his first book, *North Island Trout Fishing Guide*, in 1989. *South Island Trout Fishing Guide* followed a year later. In addition, John has written twenty-six short stories for *Rod & Rifle* magazine.

Fly Fishing Etiquette in New Zealand

*A*s there is a wide variety of water to fish in New Zealand, angling etiquette may vary accordingly. For example, fishing the mouth of a stream on Rotorua Lake or Lake Taupo is very different from sight fishing on a clear Southland stream. When sight fishing on clear rivers, the angler already in the water fishing must be allowed 3 to 4 hours of fishing water. An angler fishing in New Zealand may cover 1 kilometer per hour of river, i.e. 0.6 mile. In 3 to 4 hours of fishing time, the angler will cover 3 to 4 km or 2.5 miles. The trout population is much lower than in the U.S.A., and an angler may well cover 1 kilometer every hour. In some cases, it may be preferable to simply find another stream in the vicinity.

Of course, when the trout population is high, such as in the Tongariro River, angling pressure is much greater. Naturally, an incoming angler must not disturb another angler's fishing water. In general, if a pool is already being fished downstream, the incoming angler should start upstream, fishing away from the angler already in the water. And similarly, if a pool is being fished upstream, the newcomer should start downstream. If in doubt, always ask the anglers already fishing.

At stream mouths, always join other anglers at the end of the line unless there is an obvious gap. When there is a gap, ask neighboring anglers if it is okay to take that spot. Never move into a gap created by an angler playing or landing a fish.

Always give an angler playing a fish plenty of room. This may even mean reeling in your line until the fish has been landed. Try not to disturb other anglers' water by excessive or noisy wading, and do not walk close to the riverbank when an angler is fishing close by.

When night fishing, keep the beam of your flashlight sized to its minimum. It may not disturb the fish, but some anglers object. Finally, watch your backcast, and conversely, do not impede others by straying within casting range.

Access to most rivers and lakes in New Zealand is comparatively easy, as the Queens' Chain applies to most waterways [1 chain is 22 yards]. This is a legal right for the public to walk riverbanks and lake frontages, provided there is public access to that river or lake. Riparian rights are unusual in this country, and very little private water exists. If there is no public access, permission must be obtained from the landowner. This is seldom denied unless farming operations such as lambing are in progress. Gates must be left as found, and thanks offered on the way out.

It is essential to be conversant with the local fish and game regulations as these vary from district to district. In New Zealand, not all rules are printed on licenses, but regulations are easily obtained from local Fish and Game Councils. A New Zealand license covers the whole of the country, except for the Taupo region, where a separate license is required.

The majority of foreign anglers find that the most difficult aspect of fishing in New Zealand is spotting fish. We recommend that visiting anglers hire a professional guide, at least initially.

There are some good fly shops in the main cities, but they are not as comprehensive as the ones in the States yet. They are just adequate.

One should make reservations at least six months in advance to be on the safe side. The Taupo area is regulated separately. License fees for tourists are the same as for the locals in New Zealand.

With respect to conservation management, Trout Unlimited has a chapter in the North Island, but there are no successful ones in the South yet. There are some small conservation organizations and fishing clubs in the main cities and some small town centers located in popular fishing areas. Unfortunately, catch and release is not always practiced here.

CHRISTOPHER ROWNES
Basel, Switzerland

Christopher Rownes, born in 1966 in Wolverhampton, England, works as a contemporary dancer, choreographer, and dance teacher. He began fly fishing at the age of eight on the small streams of England and Wales. Rownes is certified as a fly casting instructor by the FFF, both in America and Europe. He is a founding member of the Board of Governors of the Commission Nacional de Lanzado in Spain. He translated and adapted into German *The Essence of Flycasting* by Mel Krieger.

Organic Degreaser

After the demise of a turbulent four-year relationship with a long-legged ballet dancer with the face of an angel and the temperament of a Spanish torero, in decadent Berlin, Germany, I decided to mourn her decline with an all out fly fishing tour of Wales, with the brand new car we had just bought together. I caught the ferry from Hamburg and sailed over to Harwich in England.

I made my way to Wales to fish the best rivers of the principality, happily smoking in our non-smoker car and enjoying every minute of it. I found a quaint little camp site right next to the river Usk. I pitched my tent next to the river and made myself at home.

I observed the river, mentally planning how I would fish the hatch later that evening. After a very strenuous morning, I decided to take a nap.

I woke up in the best of spirits, carefully prepared my equipment, pulled on my waders, and made my way to the river. I fished this new stretch of pristine river with dexterity and finesse, using the new fly fishing methods I had acquired on the rivers in Germany.

Nothing!

I persevered and made my way up the river desperately trying to find the Zen in my fly casting. I saw the monks of the Buddhist temples in Kyoto in Japan in my mind, patiently cleaning and raking the stones of their gardens and finding their way to inner peace and enlightenment. I envisaged myself as an ancient Japanese archer whose philosophy is that the archer himself becomes the target and the target becomes the archer. I sent out a cast to the target and got caught in a tree. I fought to free my fly.

"Had any luck?" were the quiet words which came over my shoulder. Startled, I looked around to see who would dare to disturb my meditation.

A glowing, red, sunburnt little man dressed in shorts, flip-flops and a string vest had been making his way delicately over to me from the camp site on the other side of the river.

"Not much," I said, thinking to myself, Poor soul—how could a normal holiday maker have the slightest glimmer of the lore and etiquette of our fly fishing world? I decided to take pity on him.

"The river seems lifeless," I said.

"Do you mind if I have a try?" he asked.

I passed him the rod as I envisaged trying to find a new rod tip for the rod tip he was just about to break in this remote area.

"Nice rod," he said, putting it between his teeth and getting down on all fours, and making his way on his hands and knees over the bare stones.

I thought to myself, I have come all this way to be alone in one of the most out-of-the-way places you can imagine, and some lunatic is crawling with my rod in mouth along the riverbank.

He approached a likely-looking spot as if it were an army enemy camp, he stripped line off the reel and a made a roll cast from a crouching position, and then he turned around and said in a quiet voice, "The leader is not sinking! Have you got any degreaser?"

"No," I said.

He turned back, waved the rod up and down vertically, and caught the leader in his left hand (to my amazement). He spat in the dirt and made a concoction of dirt, spit, and a near by cowpat; then he applied the organic mixture to the leader and made a new cast.

"That's better," he said.

With each cast, the fly landed closer to the undercut bank and sailed down the river drag-free until it was fished out. On the third cast, the leader jerked, and he was into 20 inches of wild brown trout. With absolute astonishment I watched, helpless, as the holiday maker landed my trout.

"The big fish are all tucked under the banks on this river. Your turn," he said, passing me the rod.

I swallowed and thought, There is no way I can reproduce the wizardry I have just been privileged to watch.

"I am not going home till you catch a fish," he said with a wink.

True to his word, he stayed with me, introducing me to downstream fishing his way. Almost immediately I had a strike under his guidance, but I set the hook too quickly and pulled the fly out of the fish's mouth. He advised me to wait until the fish had turned back down toward his secret lie, after taking the fly, before setting the hook.

Fifteen minutes later, I caught my first wild brown trout from the Usk. That night we fished together sharing the one rod, stalking our way downstream. Slowly it got dark and we bade each other good night.

I made my way back to my tent and opened up a beer. I watched the stars that shine almost too brightly when one is away from the lights of the city and mulled over the last three hours I had spent with a complete stranger, just our passion for fly fishing and nature connecting us.

I thought to myself how this man had approached me, with stealth and calmness. I had hardly heard him coming. He had spoken to me in a respectful and interested manner, and he had shown great respect and etiquette toward me. I swore to myself to keep an open mind to the lore and etiquette of each individual.

I turned in for the night.

Next morning I crossed the old Roman bridge over the river to visit my new-found friend, but alas, his tent was gone.

Concepts of Fly-Fishing Etiquette

Behave Calmly and Respectfully

*E*tiquette is an extremely important part of fly fishing. The etiquette fly fishers show to one another is one of the things that distinguishes fly fishing from other sports.

It is through the courtesy we show to other people that we communicate our respect for them.

The Japanese greet each other by bowing. Bowing techniques range from a small nod of the head to a long, 90 degree bow. A simple and respectful nod of the head to a fellow fly fisher while fishing is usually preferable to an awkward bowing attempt.

The tigers of Siberia mark their territory by spraying and later by hugging and rubbing the trees, leaving their strong body odor to ward off intruders. A fly fisher spraying and hugging a tree is not a pretty sight! Talk, and show respect, to fellow fly fishers. It pays big dividends.

There are a few rules of etiquette that apply in all situations and circumstances, at least in the places in Europe where I fish.

1. **Safety.** The first and foremost rule of fly fishing and fly fishing etiquette is safety. This rule applies to young and old alike. Without some good common sense, a river can be a very dangerous place.

Don't cast when someone is behind you, and don't walk around when someone is casting.

Wade the river carefully and thoughtfully, and show respect for the other fishermen around you.

2. **Approach.** If you have to approach other fishermen while they are fishing, do so in a respectful manner. Try to put yourself in their situation: Imagine you have been waiting half an hour for that old brown trout to rise again. You are all set to catch that fish of a lifetime and some gorilla with a fly rod and waders on jumps in the river in front of you! There is nothing worse than a fight on the river.

3. **Quiet.** Keep your voice down. Walk, don't run.

4. **Nature.** Treat all living creatures and the wonder of nature with respect.

5. **Keep your eyes open.** Every now and then, take time out while fishing to observe the nature around you. Sometimes we get so engrossed in our fishing that we become totally unaware of our surroundings.

My Views on Fly Fishing Today

Each year I teach people how to fly cast, the majority of whom are professional men. I look back each year and wonder to myself, Where is our future in fly fishing? Will fly fishing completely die out because the younger generation is more interested in computer games than in nature?

I always come to the same conclusion. How can we expect them to be interested in fly fishing if they are not introduced to it? Fly fishing remains to this day as exclusive as it was in the days of Halford and Skues.

Recently on a trip to visit my fellow fly casting instructor and friend Carlos in Navarra in the north of Spain, I was fascinated how one stretch of river had such a large population of fish. "That's a nice spot," I said.

"Yes, great isn't it?" he said, "That's our stretch of river reserved for school children from all over the area. Here we introduce them first of all to nature, birds, plants, trees, insects and later to fly fishing. It is a great success." Later, he showed me large stretches of the river which are free to fish with a catch and release policy. I was blown away. I thought, This is the future: simple education for the good of all and nature.

I think it is absolutely imperative that we lose the elitist attitude in fly fishing. We have to make fly fishing available to all and to awaken an interest in fly fishing amongst young people.

Once I was privileged to take a fly casting workshop in Spain with Mel Krieger. The night before the course, all the participants met in a beautiful Spanish hotel with a great bar and an open fire. When Mel introduced himself and his assistant, Rhea Topping, his opening line was: "I am already disappointed with you all."

His words were translated into Spanish and a deadly silence filled the room. Someone plucked up the courage to ask, "Why?"

Mel replied, "You are fifteen men, you have all brought your wives and children with you, and not one of them is taking the course tomorrow. I want to see all you ladies and children with a rod in your hand tomorrow."

With big eyes, they all nodded back.

Next morning, they were all there—with rods in their hands and with great enthusiasm. After two days of Mel's and Rhea's instruction they had all learnt to fly cast. As we all know, women cast with finesse and not power like men.

Mel asked me to assist him with some translations as he

walked around and instructed each individual. He whispered to me, "Look how well that woman can cast. She is better than her husband."

"Great loops," I replied.

He said, "She only started casting two days ago."

We made our way over to her to give her a compliment. Mel said, "You can cast amazingly well for just two days."

Her husband who was standing next to her casting overheard the conservation and said proudly, "She learnt everything from me."

TOMONORI HIGASHI
Yokohama, Japan

Tomonori Higashi is a teacher, an education counselor, and a magazine editor. "Tomo," or "Bill," as he is affectionately called by his American friends, has been instrumental in translating into Japanese many American fly fishing books and videos, not the least of which are all of Mel Krieger's works, *L.L. Bean Fly Fishing for Bass Handbook* and *L.L. Bean Fly-Fishing Handbook* by Dave Whitlock, and *A Different Angle* (edited by Holly Morris), in addition to numerous fly fishing articles.

Fly Fishing Customs in Japan

*S*ince the early 1980s, Western fly fishing has really taken off here. But Japan is simply too small to accommodate all of our fly fishers. Inevitably, stocked farm ponds sprouted up everywhere.

At one of the more popular ponds, I once tallied 200 anglers before I stopped counting. It was absurd, almost surrealistic, and this on a pond the size of a small soccer field. My friend informed me that this was quite a normal sight. I began to fly fish for rainbows quite often on these overcrowded farm ponds, and consequently, I witnessed and was personally involved in many problematic situations. I learned from these experiences. Eventually I came up with my own personal set of rules, which I would like to share with you, in case you should visit Japan and have the opportunity to fish one of our crowded ponds. I hope that they will be of help to you.

1. **If you are forced to fish in a corner, make short casts.** Can you guess why? Usually our ponds are square, and if you should be situated in one of the corners, you will have little room to fish on an average cast. Sandwiched between anglers on your right and left, your space will be about ten square feet. It is not productive to use a sinking line or nymphs. The only solution is to bobber fish with heavily

weighted bugger-type flies. You cast a very tight line and keep everything tight so the slightest touch of a fish on the falling fly can be detected. Once the fly hangs vertically from the bobber, you retrieve some to lift the fly and then repeat the process. Sometimes anglers use bare hooks . . . red or gold ones work especially well!

2. **If you want a good spot, get there early.** The regular anglers in these ponds like to secure their positions with aluminum chairs, making it impossible to rotate positions. I think it is a shame, but hey, Japan used to be a feudal country, and land was especially revered. I cannot blame these anglers. Although they don't rotate, there is never any trouble. They just compete to arrive earlier and take the nicer spots.

3. **If you are facing people, make short casts.** Usually, the ponds are very small. If you try to shoot out long lines, you will catch an angler instead of a fish, because you fish face-to-face. When I first started to go to these ponds, I thought I could fish and practice casting at the same time. I soon discovered that that was virtually impossible. The best advice I can give is to draw an imaginary line and fish within this area. It seems to me that most people observe this rule, but in some instances it might just be because they can't cast any farther. Admittedly, one can be easily spoiled, and long casts aren't required due to the massive numbers of stocked fish.

4. **Watch every backcast!** Usually, ponds are very crowded, and one fishes elbow-to-elbow. Your backcast might tangle with someone else's, or worse, hook a person. Because many ponds are built to use up most of the available space, there is limited space for a backcast anyway. Innocent people stroll around to see how many fish you have caught, and they even peek in your creel, if you have one.

When I teach students, I instruct them to look back to watch their loop formations and to be aware of where the fly is. At the same time, I explain that they should not look at their backcasts in an actual fishing situation. However, it seems to me that I have to change when fishing these ponds. It is practical and safe to observe every backcast at these ponds. I often fish on the natural lakes, which are less crowded and allow more space for your backcast. But one time I actually hooked a creature on my backcast. Shoot, I told myself, I hope it is not too bad. A second later, I discovered I had hooked a dog—an Afghan hound—and I was into my backing in no time.

These rules are pretty localized, I know. And some aspects of our Japanese style of fly fishing may seem absurd to you. They are the products of compromise, though. Japanese anglers have had to adjust to fly fishing in small spaces. We have no choice.

Part Seven
A WAY OF LIFE

"The environment on many of the rivers in the West is not essentially any different from that which you can see any day on upper Broadway in New York, Market Street in San Francisco, or Sunset Strip in Los Angeles. Just because people have gotten used to it and the younger fishermen have never known anything else, and therefore accept it as normal, doesn't mean it's right."

—Russell Chatham

Tom McGuane
McLeod, Montana

McGuane is a family man, a horseman, a rancher, a novelist, and, according to Jonathan Yardley in *The New York Times Book Review,* "a virtuoso . . . a writer of the first magnitude."

As the author of over ten books, Nick Lyons says of his writing talents, "No one writes with more wit and perception about the fly fishing passion. Fishing is an infallible lens through which he views the world . . . and himself."

Noted author Jim Harrison states, "Without hyperbole, McGuane writes better about fishing than anyone else in the history of mankind."

From *The Longest Silence,* Alfred A. Knopf, 2000

From the chapter entitled "Some Remarks"

I live near the great theme park of fly fishing, the headwaters of the Missouri, but go there less and less. I spend more time on the prairie rivers with their unstable banks and midsummer thermal problems. What do I find there besides a few fish that have been leading exceedingly private lives? I find solitude, which is not, take note, the same thing as loneliness.

The sport of angling used to be a genteel business, at least in the world of ideals, a world of ladies and gentlemen. These have been replaced by a new set of paradigms: the bum, the addict, and the maniac. I'm afraid this says much about the times we live in. The fisherman now is one who defies society, who rips lips, who drains pools, who takes no prisoners.

Correct spacing on a river.

Granted, he releases what he catches, but in some cases, he strips the quarry of its perilous soul before tossing it back in the water. What once was a trout—cold, hard, spotted, and beautiful—becomes "number seven."

I'm afraid the best angling is always a respite from burden. Good anglers should lead useful lives, and useful lives are marked by struggle, and difficulty, and even pain.

Therefore, bow your back and fish when you can. When you get to the water you will be renewed. Leave as much behind as possible. Those motives to screw your boss or employees, cheat on your spouse, rob the state, or humiliate your companions will not serve you well if you expect to be restored in the eyes of God, fish, and the river, which will reward you with hollow waste if you don't behave. You may be cursed. You may be shriven. You may be drowned. At the very least, you may snap your fly off in the bushes.

―――

"Uncle Ben, was my father a good fisherman?"

"No, Tommy, he was not. But no one loved it more." This to me is a conundrum. "No one loved it more."

Isn't that enough?

We have reached the time in the life of the planet, and humanity's demands upon it, when every fisherman will have to be a river keeper, a steward of marine shallows, a watchman of the high seas. We are beyond having to put back what we have taken out. We must put back more than we taken out. We must make holy war on the enemies of aquatic life as we have against gill-netters, polluters, and drainers of wetlands. Otherwise, as you have already learned, these creatures will continue to disappear at an accelerating rate. We will lose as much as we have lost already and there will be next to nothing, remnant populations, put-and-take, dim bulbs following the tank truck.

Recently I heard an old friend saying that the two rules of life he followed were: don't tell your mother your fishing spots, and other fishermen are the number one enemy. It is embarrassing to note the ring of truth these rules seem to have. But I think we're going to have to rise above them.

Early on, I decided that fishing would be my way of looking at the world. First it taught me how to look at rivers. Lately it has been teaching me how to look at people, myself included. To the reader accustomed to the sort of instructional fishing writing which I myself enjoy, I must seem to have gotten very far afield. I simply feel that the frontier of angling is no longer either technical or geographical. The Bible tells us to watch and to listen. Something like this suggests what fishing ought to be about: using the ceremony of our sport and passion to arouse greater reverberations within ourselves.

From the chapter entitled "Izaak Walton"

The technocracy of modern angling has not been conducive to the actual reading of Walton. Today's fisherman may own "The Compleat Angler" as an adornment, but turns to his bludgeoning gadgets for real twentieth-century consolation, staring at the forms of fish on the gas plasma screen of his fathometer or applying his micrometer to the nearly invisible copolymers of his leader. In Walton's words, his heart is no longer fitted for quietness and contemplation. Even in the seventeenth century there was need of a handbook for those who would overcome their alienation from nature. In our day, when this condition is almost endemic, it requires a "Silent Spring" or "The End of Nature" to penetrate our stupefaction. The evolution of angling has reached a precipice beyond which the solace, exuberance, and absorption that has sustained fishermen from the beginning will have to come from the way the art is perceived.

And here, learned, equitable Izaak Walton, by demonstrating how watchfulness and awe may be taken within from the natural world, has much to tell us; that is, less about how to catch fish, than about how to be thankful that we may catch fish. He tells us how to live.

From the chapter entitled "Roderick Haig-Brown"

For many who regard angling as the symptom of a way of living rather than a series of mechanical procedures, the writing of Roderick Haig-Brown serves as scripture.

He tried to define the space we give to angling in our lives, and to determine its value, by finding its meaning in his own life. Haig-Brown discovered that the meaning of fishing lies more in its context than its practice: a day alone on a remote steelhead river; floating with your child; fishing a lake with your family when picnic preparations overpower the angler's concentration; seeking a fish whose race is threatened by your own or whose ancestral breeding grounds have been lost to town crooks. Fishing is sometimes about a disinclination to go fishing at all. An important part of life, maybe the most important part, is the quest by each of us to discover something we believe to be more worthy and permanent than we are individually. Haig-Brown persuades us that the truth which angling can lead to about our place in nature is one such greater thing.

Sixty million disorganized fishermen are being hornswaggled by tightly organized and greedy elites. Still we cast a mistrustful eye on one another, like worn-out, secretive prospectors of last century's gold camps. The world goes on without us, using our rivers for other than their original purposes. We really ought to get together.

Jerry Kustich
Twin Bridges, Montana

Jerry Kustich has spent the past eleven years building bamboo rods. In addition to writing and illustrating a weekly nature column for a Montana newspaper, he has written magazine articles and coauthored *Fly Fishing for Great Lakes Steelhead: An Advanced Look at an Emerging*

Fishery with his brother, Rick. His recent book *At the River's Edge* chronicles many lessons learned on the life-long journey of a devoted fly angler.

P.S. Out Fishing
A Call for Common Courtesy On and Off the Stream
From *Fly Fisherman*

*T*he framed poem at the bamboo shop dangles among various pieces of memorabilia acquired through years of gathering, a lifetime of mementos donated from here and there, given in the spirit of harmony and friendship. Our shop isn't too neat, but it is arranged with a sense of purpose. These treasures stand in the corners, decorate the walls, or just lean on something that is leaning on something else, each a source of inspiration to all who take the time to look. The forgotten verse that once adorned a general hardware and sporting goods store in Columbus, Nebraska, in the 1920s hangs almost hidden from view under years of accumulated dust. But for anyone interested enough to read it, the modest words reach out with an insightfulness still relevant to the modern-day angler.

> *Out Fishing*
> A feller isn't thinking mean,
> Out fishing,
> His thoughts are mostly good and clean,
> Out fishing,
> He doesn't mock his fellow men,
> Or harbor any grudges then;
> A feller's at his finest when,
> Out fishing,

The rich are comrades to the poor,
Out fishing,
All are brothers of a common lure,
Out fishing,
The urchin with his pin and string,
Can chum with millionaire or king;
Vain pride is a forgotten thing,
Out fishing,
A feller gets a chance to dream
Out fishing.
He learns the beauties of the stream out fishing.
And he can wash his soul in air
That isn't foul with selfish care,
And relish plain and simple fare
Out fishing,
A feller has no time to hate,
Out fishing,
He isn't eager to be great
Out fishing,
He isn't thinking thoughts of self,
Or goods stacked high upon his shelf,
But he's always just himself,
Out fishing.
[A] feller's glad to be a friend, out fishing.
[A] helping hand he'll always lend, out fishing.
The brotherhood of rod and line
An' sky and stream is always fine;
Men come real close to God's design, out fishing.

Such humble truth, I thought, when I first read it. In fact, the
verse not only captured the very spirit of those fly anglers

Too close for comfort—even if they are married.

whom I have most admired over the years, but with childlike simplicity it also expressed all the hidden reasons I fish, for which I had no words. In an effort to share this revelation with those convinced my life had run amok in the trivial pursuit of an idle pastime, I took the poem home to show my wife.

"Kind of sexist, don't you think?" Her first response caught me off guard.

Though I realized it could be interpreted that way, I replied by shaking my head and saying, "It was written way back when." Stammering a bit, I quickly added, "Men were expected to be sexist in those days. They invented the concept."

Then I got on my pulpit. "I'm sure Mr. Unknown would have been astute enough to be politically sensitive if he wrote his poem in the late 1990s. Heck, maybe Ms. Unknown wrote it. Who knows? The point is that the message holds as much insight for gals as it does for fellers. Make a few generic changes. Just substitute 'they're' for 'he's' and 'theirs' for 'his,' etc. In other words, bring it up to code and it still rings true, don't you think?" Although it wasn't Shelley or Yeats, Debra was willing to admit that it was a quaint piece—if only in a down-home sort of way.

So there I was a few weeks later, fishing to five consistent bank feeders in the Missouri River on a morning marked by a stiff breeze and very few tricos. The hours beforehand had been a bust. Since a dry, cold front had set in the night before, cool Canadian air descended on the Craig area in the form of uncomfortable gusty winds. Consequently, a thorough search of several stretches revealed absolutely no surface activity anywhere on the rippled water. At least this little oasis tucked against the willows provided ample windbreak to make a few close but erratic casts to several nice browns surface sipping close to the bank in about a foot or less of water.

After wading 30 feet out into the knee-deep current while working upstream to calculate the proper angle, I started my tactical assault toward the shallows. Intensely engaged in the ritual of casting, changing flies, and casting again, I barely heard the sloshing of an approaching angler as he dragged his drift boat upstream a mere few hundred feet below where I stood.

When he got within earshot, he announced, "Excuse me, I'm going to have to walk through your water." Before I could answer, he added quickly, "But I'll do so quietly."

"What?" My not too unreasonable response stung the morning chill. "You have got to be kidding."

"You got a problem with that?" His words skipped back across the water with a tone of rancor. Then, as if cloaked politeness could possibly excuse this intrusion, his tack changed to an unctuous retort, "Hey, I asked you nicely."

My mind flashed immediately to an incident earlier in the year on the Bitterroot when two passing anglers could not resist bombarding Stimulators to the same lone rising cutthroat to which I was casting from a difficult position in the river. In fact, the oarsman had to make a quick maneuver to avoid wiping me out. I didn't say a word.

Then there was the young guide who walked his boat full of clients through a stretch of rising fish on the Madison last year, barely acknowledging my presence. I didn't say a word then either.

And I also didn't say a word when an angler stopped his kick-boat at the head of a run on the Big Hole and proceeded to start casting downstream to the same pod of risers I was carefully working just 30 feet below him. It only took a few double hauls from his bullet-quick rod before the fish disappeared. He then got back into his one-man vessel and floated by. "Well, I guess I spooked them," were the only words that seeped through a wry smirk.

Integrity is a difficult concept to define. We talk about it all the time at the bamboo shop. It has something to do with being truthful to oneself and respectful to others—really quite simple. Though a basic Christian precept, there are even some faithful followers in every church who don't quite get it either. But in an era of virtual reality, nothing is what it seems anymore. Lawyers have seen to that. With straight faces, tobacco company representatives claim cigarettes aren't harmful to one's health, Rodney King gets pummeled on videotape while his offenders are exonerated, and surreptitiously our perception of truth begins to erode.

Then there's Ollie North, O. J. Simpson, Bill Clinton, Monica Lewinsky, and even Kenneth Starr—from the top on down, we get the sense that integrity is no longer what it used to be. Kids learn to kill on video games. And when they actually do, we are all shocked, yet gamemakers claim no responsibility. Heck, we can't even elect a president without doubting the truthfulness of the process as interpreted by a politically biased court system.

No wonder truth is fuzzy these days and integrity smells like a pair of old gym socks. It seems that we have entered the age of smoke and mirrors, and what you see isn't what you get. Increasingly, the artificial becomes real, and the manipulated truth we are dealt looks more and more like the world according to the World Wrestling Federation.

In an honest effort to get back to the basics, perhaps I constantly seek a river seam of primordial holy water to cleanse away all the deceptions of a misguided society and the deleterious effects these attitudes have on the human spirit.

Somewhere, ebbing forth from the soul of Mother Earth, there has to be a message of substance appropriate for the times. And in the process of searching for trout I hope to grasp the tag end of an unraveling thread that leads back to the core essence of what truth is all about. But in my naiveté I have always held that every fly fisher operated on this same plane.

As essential as the rod, reel, and fly are to the angler, I also believed that integrity was the intangible bond of commonality we all shared while "out fishing." And until recent times, it never even occurred to me that the world I was trying to avoid would eventually worm its way onto the waters of contemplative refuge. Undaunted by my presence, the sloshing proceeded.

I could tell immediately that this was a feller who hadn't yet read "Out Fishing" by Mr. Unknown. As a feller who already had, I was torn between the options of mild-mannered acceptance or speaking out on behalf of downtrodden anglers everywhere who have to put up with ignorant, modern-day macho jerks trying to pass themselves off as God's gift to the fishing world. In my mind the debate continued as the ominous figure relentlessly closed the remaining space between us.

Since there was no apparent emergency motivating the boatman's activity, I declared to myself that enough was enough. The free-for-all prevalent on many of our Western rivers these days needs a David-type leader to beat the burgeoning Goliath back into submission. In an instant I made up my mind. This time I was most definitely going to say a word. "Yeah. I have a big problem with that." My reply of conviction rang on behalf of every decent gal and feller who ever sought sanctuary in a quiet corner of mind and water with a fly rod in hand.

I then started my diatribe. "Look, I chose this out-of-the-way spot so I wouldn't be bothered by drift boats. A drift boat is for drifting, anyway, not dragging, and especially not through water someone is peacefully fishing. It would seem that the boat should allow you access to much more river than this little stretch I have available to me. Or am I missing something?" I then suggested we consider some alternatives.

"Why are you being such an a—hole?" The reply was blunt. He then continued. "I'm going through. Those fish will be back feeding in five minutes. You idiots from the city don't know anything about these Missouri River fish. Go the f—k back to where you belong."

The ensuing verbal exchange would have embarrassed Mr. Unknown, and, I am sorry to say, it certainly did trash the whole spirit of his piece. At the intruder's behest, we could have settled the entire matter with our fists, but I laughed at the inane suggestion.

In the end, I helplessly watched as the indignant boat owner draped a rope over his shoulder and puffed the wooden craft through the rising fish. He cast aspersions all the way upriver until he was out of hearing distance. I didn't stay around long enough to see if those browns would have come back to feed, which really wasn't the point.

About two holes upriver the interloper boarded the boat. He then rowed across, got out, and started to fish in an out-of-the-way side channel where most likely he would not be bothered by another soul. For his own convenience, he inconvenienced me—a monumental irony lost on the self-absorbed. And since his power of observation must have been skewed by the massive dose of testosterone that apparently had shriveled his brain, he was sure wrong about me.

I live in a town of 300 people and look like I just came down from the mountains. However, his attitude would have definitely been offensive to any visiting urban dweller. More disturbing, his actions poorly represented most other Montanans who are ethical, good natured "non-city types."

Out of nowhere this unenlightened nonfeller appeared, as if sent to test my spiritual aptitude. At first glance, it would seem that I failed miserably to advance to a higher plane, but there has to be some virtue in taking a principled stance.

We can spare fellow humans a lot of grief by watching out for the rights of the other guy (or gal), a lesson on the river that can be applied to the rest of life. If you are doing something that truly upsets someone else, you are probably out of line. I'd say that is a good rule of thumb.

Then there is the notion that somehow the act of fishing is close to godliness. "Out Fishing," at least, suggests this be true. Although there is no theological proof or scriptural support, it often has been said that God does not count days out fishing as a part of our total time allotted on earth. If this is correct, then the opposite may also apply to those who misbehave while out fishing. But that discussion is best left to those who are still trying to figure out what happened to all the Catholics who ate meat on Fridays and then died before the rules changed.

It is obvious that our unknown poet never had to deal with the "me first" attitude that dominates society today. If so, there undoubtedly would have been another verse or two added to his work to address such issues. I thus took the liberty to write a postscript on behalf of the original author.

> *Out Fishing*
> A feller ought to see the light,
> Out Fishing,
> There is no room to start a fight, Out Fishing.
> This silent world has truths to tell,
> There are no rainbow trout in hell;
> So treat your fellow anglers well, Out Fishing.

GARY BORGER

Wausau, Wisconsin

In addition to having been a Professor of Biology at the University of Wisconsin Center, Borger lectures internationally, is an active member of the Outdoor Writer's Association of America, the Midwest Field Editor for *Fly Fisherman* magazine, was a pioneer in the production of fly fishing videos, was a consultant on *A River Runs Through It*, and has produced an award-winning CD, *My Madison.*

He is the author of *Nymphing, Naturals, Borger Color System, Designing Trout Flies,* and *Presentation.*

A Careless Approach

*T*here are ideal days and there are *ideal* days. This was one of the *ideal* ones. A deep blue sky only heightened the ragged edges of the mountains and made the water seem all the more clear. But at the moment, these "roses" were going unsmelled. A heavy hatch of the Pale Morning Dun mayflies *(Ephemerella* *infrequens)* was busily organizing itself, and the fish had found the emerging insects. And not just any fish. The big boys were out in force and eating greedily.

Just upstream from me were three fish ranging from 20 to 24 inches in length. Their big snouts poked out time after time, busily slurping in the partially emergent duns. It was the perfect setup, and I crept forward slowly, one baby step at a time, intent on reaching the best casting position unobserved.

But such was not to be the case. However, it wasn't the fish that saw me, it was a couple of other anglers. They were walking down my side of the river, and upon spotting me, they stopped and watched for a few moments. Then, to my dismay, they marched briskly toward me. As they tromped heavily past the fish I had so carefully been stalking, the big leviathans bolted for mid-river. The anglers never saw the fish leave.

I stood up, not too happy, and politely greeted my unwelcome guests. They wanted to talk, and talk, and talk. I wanted to fish, and fish, and fish. Not that I mind talking to other anglers, but those big fish were really big. Even one of them would have made my day, and I was disappointed that I didn't get to take a couple of them on.

After the others left, I headed back to the van for lunch. I brooded a bit, but only a bit. After all, the day was lovely, and I was on the shores of one of my most favorite rivers. I lay back in the shade of the vehicle and smelled the roses. It was a delight to be alive.

But such times must necessarily be short when the hatch is still heavy. Perhaps my big finny friends had come back to feed again. I grabbed the rod and headed to my vantage point. And there they were, back and rising with just as much gusto as before. Maybe the day would prove to be a banner one after all.

Again the cautious approach: watching the big noses poke out, marking their exact holding positions, calculating the perfect placement of the fly, anticipating the head-shaking run of the lower fish as I tightened the line. And then, just as I made the intended casting position, two anglers appeared upstream. They were walking down my side of the river, and upon spotting me, they stopped and watched for a few moments. Then, to my dismay, they marched briskly toward me. As they tromped heavily past the fish I had so carefully been stalking, the big leviathans bolted for mid-river. The anglers never saw the fish leave.

Twice was just too much. I turned and briskly waded across the stream, leaving my companions ungreeted on the far bank. Back at the truck, I put up my gear, and then drove away. It just wasn't to be, at least not this day, at least not on this river. I was frustrated, but soon I was smelling roses again and looking for another spot where big fish might be daintily sipping tiny insects from the surface film.

But the story doesn't end here; no, it actually begins here. A couple of months later I received a vitriolic letter from an angler who had been on the river that day. He accused me of being a snob, of "looking down my sunglasses" at the other anglers, of being the worst of cads. I was a bit nonplused. Wasn't I the one who should have felt angry? Wasn't I the one who should have given my uninvited fish-spooking guests a good dressing down at their total lack of etiquette? Wasn't the right on my side?

Well, perhaps, but then I realized that my etiquette had not been much better either. I had created enemies where enemies should not exist. I had dulled someone else's edge and had caused them frustration and anger that obviously had lasted for a long time. Such things should not exist in fly fishing. So I wrote a letter of apology and explained the situation, a situation they could not possibly have known about. It was cathartic for me to have a chance to gently tell others that all anglers, no matter how long or short they've fished, nor how well they may be known or unknown, still have the need for a bit of space—especially when working to rising fish. I can only hope they understood.

"*The world of angling is richly diverse. . . . It elicits some of the sweetest and deepest qualities in man—and, occasionally, some of the worst. It can be coolly dispassionate, lyrical, or maddeningly intense.*"

—Nick Lyons

Nick Lyons
New York, New York

Angler, man of letters, gentleman of gentlemen, Lyons for many years ran his own publishing company, Nick Lyons Books, where he rescued a number of classic fishing books from obscurity and put them back into print. He has written several books of his own, as well as numerous magazine articles, and for several years he contributed a monthly column to *Fly Fisherman* magazine. He divides his time between New York City and the Catskills.

Crowds

From *The Flyfisher's World*
The Atlantic Monthly Press, 1995

$\mathcal{T}$hey're wonderful, I suppose, if you're selling something—from snake oil to books to religion to hard rock. And you can't have a political rally for the best—or worst—of causes without them. They are the fodder and the clout of revolutions, the pulse and chorus of great sporting events, comfort and protection for all those who are afraid to act except in concert. But have you ever heard a serious fly fisher sing their glory?

There is a bit of moving water, a few rising trout, and you. That's where all value begins in fly fishing. A bit of moving water, a few rising trout, and ten people are a bad joke.

In the past ten years or so we've seen a huge increase in the number of fly fishers everywhere. A lot of folk refer to "The Movie" as the greatest ambassador—or shill—for the sport, and perhaps, if we forget what the book stood for, it has been that. There are lots more books today, too, some of which sell in numbers not previously imagined—while other decent ones vanish simply because there are too many titles vying for attention, crowding the magazine reviews, tackle stores, and patience of anglers.

Fly fishing is also the subject of more and more fashionable ads, and even I (surely the adult with the least possible style, or interest in it) have been asked by companies like Ralph Lauren for tips on how the upper end of the fly fishing world attires itself for the sport; I could only laugh uncontrollably and send them elsewhere. Rods and reels and lines are more efficient. Flies are more cunning, making entry-level work more manageable. And a lot more time has been spent to dress the newcomer in a happy uniform (pink waders for new women fly fishers go too far).

Schools proliferate and are filled to capacity. Newspapers like the *New York Times* have run front-page articles on salmon fishing in Russia and the growing number of women fly fishers. The cable television shows take us everywhere and with careful editing can make us think it's heaven on that mosquito-ridden little island . . . and even major news/essay programs think it's all-important enough to carry a "segment."

Fly fishing is everywhere—even where we could not have dreamed it would go: parodies, in the *Boston Globe* and the *New Yorker,* of fishing memoirs; and a recent article in a women's magazine showing a batch of young, ruggedly handsome male fly-fishing guides, who are possible "catches" for the young, bright, pretty women who read that rag.

Lots of folks who have loved fly fishing for many years, and have wanted to share it, suddenly discover that the indifferent neighbor now can't get enough of it. And the parameters continue to grow with the emergence of great travel agencies that explore the world, finding new possibilities in New Zealand, the Pacific, Africa, Russia, and where not else. "It looks like so much fun," a young friend told me recently. "Will you teach me?" I hesitated.

My friend Steven Meyers, in his *San Juan River Chronicle,* speaks of it as "a river in danger of being loved to death."

And there, on a specific river, is where the problem comes home the hardest: will it bear all the love we want to crowd upon it?

Anyone who's fished for a substantial time—I'm beyond fifty years now—continues to feel that steady, inescapable erosion of waters know earlier.

I fished a river two hours from New York a hundred times in my childhood, a back section, meandering from a hillside under a railroad trestle, through a broad meadow, making a few sharp turns, and then sliding past a small town. It was a stream uniformly some sixty feet across, with deep water in all but a few spots, soft undercut banks, hundreds of deadfalls. It was never an easy river to fish, because the bordering trees threw a low canopy across it, you could only wade the edges, and it was always slightly discolored from its movements through farm country. But there were five miles of it that I fished, and it always stunned me with its surprises: once, the largest trout I have ever taken in the East, a five- or six-pound brown. Because the water wasn't easy to fish and because it had superb cover with the tangled branches of the deadfalls, the river produced a large number of outsized brooks and browns—and few people fished it after mid-April. I did a number of times and never caught a lot of fish, but I always raised a few tortugas. I went back to it five years ago and found in the meadow no fewer than three or four hundred small houses, all looking pretty much the same. I haven't seen it since.

Mostly it has been the raw need (or greed) for some places to develop, or pollute, that has wrecked the waters I love—but increasingly it's the sheer number of fly fishers.

There is a bridge over a western river near where I used to park some years ago. The water was tough, heavy, but it held very good trout, and a lot of them. I fished it ten or fifteen times when I was the only person in sight, and then, as the years went on, I found other spots. One day recently I went back with Mari, who wanted to paint there, and my son Paul, with whom I wanted to share this exceptional spot, and I could barely control my rage. They thought I'd gone berserk or gotten bitten by a wasp when I came over the hill and looked down to the bridge: there were no fewer than seventy or eighty cars there. I've never fished it since.

I can remember a dozen places—far back through weed, swamp, bramble patches—where a particular confluence of currents, a bend in the river, and a bottom dug out by the force of the flow combined to create a true "honey hole," a place bound to contain fish—a place that, time after time, did hold good fish.

If you fuss around rivers long enough, you find a lot of places like this, often just a bit farther from roads and access points than most folks care to go. You break through the tangle of brush one day by chance, after a dozen fruitless forays searching, and discover a secret garden that rewards you with remarkable riches. You go back . . . same thing. And then, as the entire river gets more pressure, you make the same unpleasant hour long trek through the swamp that eats waders, get bitten by mosquitoes, have your net catch on a bush and thorns and then slam into your back, lose a box of your best flies and the whole contraption that holds clippers, fly dope, hemostat, and you find there are four lunatics there. They are fishing hard, wading in the wrong places, shouting over the sound of water, spooking fish, and pounding the water to a frenzy, and you never have the heart to go back.

Or it's a spot to which you must wade through dangerous waters, for half an hour, and when you brave it this time and lift your head, you see a McKenzie boat has just lightly deposited two anglers exactly on the bar from which you have always fished.

Home waters become everyone's waters; a favorite spot

becomes a public meeting place; and you feel tugged to hunt a receding new, or as several old friends have done, just stop. Give it up. Leave the field. One took up golf and loves it. "The crowds just got to be too much," he told me.

Some new people will come into the sport and drift away; a lot will stay. I wish I could see some change in sight, but I'm a Jeremiah about crowds. Look at Cairns Pool on the Beaverkill, Buffalo Ford on the Yellowstone, the traffic at Varney Bridge when Mr. Salmonfly has arrived . . . any of us could name a couple dozen more.

The crowds will only increase, I'm afraid. We'll have to start thinking hard about some difficult, unpleasant options: exerting ourselves a lot more to avoid crowds, limiting access, finding or saving more water, and demanding of our new colleagues—before they enter a river—a bit more toilet training.

If you love fly fishing, as I do, we'll do all of the above, and more.

DOUG SWISHER AND CARL RICHARDS
Hamilton, Montana, and Rockford, Michigan

In 1970, Joe Brooks presented two young researchers in aquatic entomology and fly tying to the angling world. The following year, Swisher and Richards published their landmark *Selective Trout*, which advocated a new way of looking at flies and the ways to tie and fish them. Since then, both men have continued to make contributions to fly fishing, both in publishing and instruction. Together they also wrote *Fly Fishing Strategy* and *Emergers*.

Stream Courtesy
From *Fly Fishing Strategy,* Crown Publishers, Inc., 1975

*T*he whine of the bullet, as it sped by our ears, startled and frightened us. It had been a soft fall morning and the big Muskegon River was low, clear, and filled with steelhead, king, and silver salmon. The stillness of the morning was broken by the crashing of pistol shot. Some fishermen camped about four hundred yards upstream were calmly tossing beer cans in the flow and target shooting at them. Soon a nice string of silver cans was floating by us. The vandal sportsmen seemed to have plenty of ammunition, for the shooting continued for fully three-quarters of an hour. Originally they had been aiming upstream away from us, but now they were shooting toward our position, and a few of the slugs were ricocheting from the surface and coming very close indeed. After the near miss, we finally yelled rather impolitely for them to stop. Luckily for us they did, so we are still around to write this chapter.

Now, we realize that no chapter on stream etiquette will ever stop the idiots like these from desecrating beautiful trout streams, or from creating dangerous situations. People who do the type of thing we just described may be unreachable, and we will probably always have to put up with a certain amount of plain stupidity.

In the golden days of fly fishing, when our rivers were uncrowded and filled with 14-inch brookies and 18-inch browns, the few fishermen one did encounter on the streams were almost always a courteous group of knowledgeable people, often steeped

Bad manners: The older man is yelling at the boy to let him fish that spot.

in the tradition of the English chalk streams. They knew a wet-fly fisher working downstream must make way when approaching the more aristocratic dry-fly fisher, who always worked upstream. And they really seemed to follow these rules.

In those golden days of under population it was much easier to be courteous. It was not at all difficult to elude the three or four anglers one met in a day's outing. Dodging our fellow sportsmen these days, however, is an ever-continuing and often insurmountable problem.

Fly fishing for trout is, by its very nature, an introspective sport; it demands solitude. That is not to say that it does not produce great friendships and comrades, because it does. But when one is stalking a free-rising "good-un" with a perfect cast and a lovely float, the last thing anyone needs is some clownish dolt splashing up to you and booming, "How's the fishing?" A true answer would be, "Great until you ruined it."

Unlike those men shooting cans, many neophyte fly fishermen are discourteous out of ignorance and inexperience, rather than pure maliciousness. In these times, when even our isolated western streams are becoming very crowded, and the fly fishing methods are much more varied, stream etiquette is not as clear-cut as it once was. Dry-fly men, more often than not, fish downstream rather than following the ancients blindly. Streamer fishermen, nymphers, and wet-fly anglers often are found facing upstream, against the current, in defiance of all the old traditions. Now, who gets out of the way of whom?

The old rules then must be rewritten in light of modern conditions. If, in fact, the enjoyment of fly fishing demands at least a certain amount of solitude, the prime rule must be: Conduct yourself so as to disturb your fellow angler as little as the prevailing conditions allow.

Now these prevailing conditions will vary considerably over a season. There is no way anyone will find much solitude on most of our good trout streams on opening day. You will probably have to insert yourself between two anglers, who are already much too close together. On most rivers, that will be the only way possible to get into the water at all during the early season. During the late season, say after late June or early July, many of our great rivers are almost deserted, so there is not much of a problem finding a good pool, or even long stretches of water undisturbed.

If you are wading, and overtake a slower angler fishing in the same direction, get out of the water and walk around him. Go as far past him as reasonably possible (around a bend so as to be out of sight would be ideal) before returning to the stream. Above all, do not wade right up and start a conversation; you may disturb a pod of rising trout, and no one will appreciate such conduct.

When meeting another fisherman approaching from an opposite direction, ease around the edge of the stream, or get out if possible, as you pass. It is perfectly all right to have a pleasant conversation, as long as you do not disturb any fish within his casting range. These rules are nothing more than common sense and common courtesy, but it is truly amazing how many anglers just do not stop and think before barging in.

Nowadays, more people are floating our rivers and streams in canoes and boats. This type of fly fishing requires a slightly different set of rules. The floater should be able to handle his canoe or boat properly, and have it under control at all times. When approaching a wading angler, he should pass in back of that angler so as not to disturb the water he is working. The most discourteous act a floater can perform is to come between a wader and a fish he is casting to, and then cast out to that very same fish. It is especially annoying when the intruder actually takes the fish you have quietly stalked and are working on.

This actually happens daily on some rivers we fish. The people who perpetrate these maddening acts are mostly perfectly nice people when away from the stream. It seems that in their lust for catching fish, they leave their brains at home.

You will undoubtedly encounter many situations for which there will be no specific rule, but it all boils down to this: common courtesy and common sense in all situations, and treat the other fellow's water with the respect it deserves.

A word, also, about respecting landowners' property. If we are to have any public water left in this country, with the exception of public fishing sites, we must treat the streams we fish as we would treat our own property. Many people don't, and this creates a problem for those of us who do. Many of us from the Midwest and far West would love to pay homage to the rivers about which Flick and Schwiebert and many others have written so eloquently. But most of the best water is now private and posted. Litterbugs, fish hogs, vandals, and poachers reduced the banks to junkyards, and decimated the trout population to the point where either the public had to be excluded or the streams would not be worth fishing. Some of these rivers have returned to their old greatness. But the average angler will never tread the bans unless he has an "in."

Many western waters are owned by ranchers who love their land. They simply will not, and need not, tolerate the senseless acts that resulted in the closing of our eastern streams. Twenty years ago, you had only to ask to fish anywhere in the West you wished to fish. Today, more and more landowners are refusing permission to all but their friends. A few so-called anglers scaring cattle, leaving gates open, and littering these waters will ruin it for us all.

It is probably inevitable that someday all but a small amount of public water will be posted, and this "free" country will become similar to England and the rest of Europe; there, of course, the elite few control the fishing rights, and one must join a club or pay a day ticket, even for the chance to fish a reservoir.

Fishing waters that run through other people's land is a privilege. It is not, and probably never should have been considered a "right," in which anyone who bought a fishing license could indulge. Someday private water will almost certainly become the rule.

If we can conduct ourselves like ladies and gentlemen, perhaps we may hold off the darkness for just a little longer.

⎯⎯⟨∞⟩⎯⎯

WILLIAM G. TAPPLY
Hancock, New Hampshire

Tapply is the author of fourteen New England–based mystery novels, as well as several books about outdoor sports, including *Sportsman's Legacy* and *A Fly-Fishing Life*. He is a contributing editor for *Field & Stream*, and a columnist for *American Angler* and *Worcester Magazine*.

Bad Manners on the Water Can Ruin a Dream
from *American Angler*, 2001

June in the Catskills

A couple of weeks shy of the longest day of the year, I had set my alarm for a half-hour before sunrise, but I didn't need it. I had drifted off to sleep reviewing my memories of the Bridge Pool, and I had slept fitfully and dreamfully. I was wide awake before the alarm went off.

My dream featured a trout even larger than the actual trout I'd failed to catch from the Bridge Pool the previous June. That actual trout had been 18 or 19 inches long. Maybe 20. He'd been sipping sunrise spinners against the far bank in the shadowy eddy where a square boulder jutted into the current. I had spotted the little blip of his riseform—about the same disturbance a blueberry would make if you dropped it into the water from a height of one foot—and then spent a half-hour figuring out where to stand and how much slack to throw into the longish reach cast that was needed to drift a fly over him without drag. Once I'd found my position about a 45-degree angle upstream and across from him—I was able to spot the fish's ghostly form each time he edged away from the boulder's shadow to eat, and I measured his feeding rhythm. He was unquestionably the biggest trout I'd ever encountered on this famous—and famously overrated and overfished—trout stream.

It had taken another 15 or 20 minutes of trial and error to figure out what he was eating from the smorgasbord of spinners and spent caddisflies that drifted on the water. The trout told me when he lifted his nose and my fly—a size 20 rusty hen-wing spinner with a peacock herl thorax—drifted into his open mouth.

I hadn't expected it, of course. So my reflexes reacted instead of my brain, and I lifted my rod too quickly, plucking the fly cleanly out of his mouth.

The trout in my dream porpoised out of the water each time he ate, an arrogant head-and-shoulders rise intended to taunt me by flaunting his full length and fatness. When he rose, his eye stared directly into mine. This dream trout was at least 30 inches long. It didn't matter, because in my dream every cast fell in limp coils around my knees. He kept rising, that big eye staring at me with what might have been pity, or contempt, while I flailed around, and I could not get a cast beyond the tip of my absurd twig of a rod.

The stars were beginning to wink out and the sky over the Catskills was just fading from purple to pewter when I slipped out of the motel and into my car. The whole question was: Would I be the first angler at the Bridge Pool? On this weekend in June, the town swarmed with automobiles displaying Trout Unlimited decals on the back windows and wearing more license plates from Pennsylvania, Massachusetts, and Connecticut than from New York. I actually spotted one from Michigan and another from West Virginia.

I knew exactly where I wanted to be standing. I had a rendezvous with a trout. If not that specific big trout who had lived in the eddy behind the boulder last year, then another big trout who'd settled in the same place. There's a sweet spot in every pool, and the biggest resident trout always occupies it. I'd found that sweet spot in the Bridge Pool, which was the sweetest pool on the river.

The New York DEC had cleared a parking area overlooking the Bridge Pool, and they'd built a wooden platform over the water for handicapped anglers. The pool was no secret. Even without the amenities, you couldn't miss it. At its head, it emerged from the evergreen forest, tumbled around boulders, flowed under the bridge, then widened and deepened and slowed. It was classic.

But that sweet spot where the big trout lived—I had discovered that all by myself.

I clenched my fist and muttered "Yes" when I found the lot empty of vehicles. I'd done it. I'd beaten the crowd.

I didn't linger in the car to admire the way mist was wafting off the water or to marvel at the fingers of pink that were clawing into the sky. I leaped out, tugged on my waders, strung my rod, and waded in.

It had been a year, but the memory of it remained vivid, and I found the exact place where I had stood. I tied on a size 20 rusty spinner with a peacock herl thorax and fingered some floatant into it. Not because I believed my trout would necessarily be eating rusty spinners this morning, but for luck, and for tradition, and for lack of a better idea.

A few smallish trout splashed and spurted in front of me, but I ignored them. I focused on the shadowy eddy behind the square boulder.

The first time he rose, I thought it was my imagination, wishful thinking. The image had burned so deeply into my mind a year earlier that it had sometimes appeared when I was staring out my office window at the snow on MY lawn, or driving a highway, or falling asleep at night.

No, he was there, and when I squinted through my polarized glasses, I saw the shape of him. He could have been the same trout, grown an inch or two longer in the year since I'd yanked my fly out of his mouth.

I resisted the urge to begin casting immediately. I let him come up several times to whet his appetite and gain courage, while I gauged his rhythm.

My first cast fell short, and I slid it away before it could drag over him. On my next cast, he stuck up his nose and ate before my fly got to him.

My third cast was on the water, neatly air-mended, perfectly timed, and I knew this was the one. I reminded myself not to strike too soon when he ate my fly, to let him close his mouth and turn his head so the hook would catch in the corner of his mouth when I lifted my rod and tightened on him . . . .

That's when a length of bright yellow fly line came floating past me. When I looked up, I saw that the line was attached to a rod, and the rod was being held by a fisherman. He had waded into the Bridge Pool while I was focused on my trout, and he was now standing barely 10 feet upstream from where I stood, casting across-and-down, covering the water directly in front of me.

My first—irrational—thought was that I was still deep in my

fishing-frustration dream, that I was back in my motel room waiting for the alarm clock to wake me up.

My second thought was that if I had a gun. . . .

"Hello?" I said to the guy. "Excuse me?"

"Hi, there," he said pleasantly. "Beautiful morning, eh?" He looked to be in his early thirties. He was wearing a cowboy hat and a pair of those new breathable waders and a vest festooned with gadgets and gewgaws. I couldn't tell what kind of rod he was using, but it was a nice one, and I recognized the reel. It was a very expensive reel. It looked brand new.

"Am I invisible?" I said.

He frowned. "Huh?"

"I mean, can you see me?"

He smiled. "Oh, sure. Plain as day."

"Just checking," I said. "Am I in your way?"

"Oh, no," he said. "Don't worry about it. You're fine."

I took a deep breath. "Look," I said. "There's a nice fish right in front of me."

"What?" he said. " Where?" He ripped his line off the water in front of me, made a couple of false casts, and splashed it down beside the rock where my trout had been rising. "There?"

So I reeled in, waded out of the Bridge Pool, sat on the handicapped casting ramp, and watched that guy cast at my fish.

I couldn't decide whether to be amused or furious at his astounding lack of courtesy, at his apparent immunity to sarcasm, at the ironic predictive truth of my fishing dream.

I remembered the time some guy had come sloshing downstream to cast over a rising trout my partner was casting upstream to and how they'd ended up standing toe-to-toe debating ownership of that fish. I remembered all the times I'd nearly been run down by drift boats while wading. This wasn't the first time I'd been shouldered out of a pool I thought I had to myself.

The guy kept casting at my trout. He wasn't very skilled, and I was delighted that he didn't catch it.

I pondered some easy generalizations—how Hollywood has made fly fishing too damn popular, how the schools and shows and books and videos do a great job of teaching fly casting and entomology and knots but a lousy job of teaching manners, how contemporary society rewards competitiveness and aggressiveness and selfishness and punishes old-fashioned civility.

I'd set my alarm so I could get here first and stake my right-eous claim to the sweetest spot on the entire river.

And I'd succeeded. I'd beaten everybody. I'd won, dammit.

That was my spot, my fish. Wasn't it?

—⚬⚬⚬—

STEVE RAJEFF
Woodland, Washington

When it comes to delivering long, accurate casts or dropping a fly or a plug on a dime, nobody in the world does it better than Rajeff, Director of Research and Development at G. Loomis. He has dominated the world of competitive casting for over two decades, and he has no less than twenty-four national titles and thirteen world championships under his belt.

Much Obliged

Anglers' etiquette. Hmmmm . . . . Brother Buzz, do unto others as . . . . Yeah but, what if it's Saturday after opening day and the stream is crowded? What if all the fish are ganged up in one spot and there are already anglers on top of them? What if the guy in your favorite pool is a known jerk? What should I do if I were a guide with clients? How would I behave if I were a lodge owner? What if I travel to another country to fish: How should I act around other anglers there?

Exchanging flies.

Every situation has social obligations that may range from being rude and unacceptable if you are on the same river, bay or flat, to being downright anti-social if you are not rubbing elbows. The only way to find out if you are not being the subject of another angler's spite is to politely ask if you are encroaching.

I have never been offended by anyone who has asked how fishing was and would it be OK to move in above or below me. That is, with the exception of shallow saltwater situations, such as fishing for bonefish, where your mere presence in an area would likely ruin the fishing for the other guy.

But for the most part, in most situations, and on most waters, a friendly "howdy," and "do you mind if I go here or there?" only strengthens the bond among anglers, and contributes to the reasons why we fish.

Another aspect of angling etiquette, which I sadly see all too often ignored, is trashing the area. One of the reasons I enjoy fishing so much is it gets me to some of the most beautiful places on Planet Blue. It is really disheartening to go to a remote location and find trash, such as cigarette butts, cans, and wrappers. If we anglers would be more diligent about packing out what we pack in, I am certain that landowners would allow more access. So, please, fellow anglers: do not only your share, but also help to clean up after the more careless ones.

As angling pressure increases upon a diminishing natural resource, consider your obligation to the environment, and have respect for your fellow anglers, and the fish you pursue. Much obliged.

DENNIS SMITH
Loveland, Colorado

Smith, an outdoor writer since 1991, has published in *Colorado Outdoors, American Angler, The Flyfisher, Western Fly Fishing, Rocky Mountain Game & Fish,* and *North American Whitetail* among others. He writes three outdoor columns a month: "Up the Creek" for *Colorado Country Life* magazine; "Home Waters" for the *Loveland Daily Reporter-Herald;* and "Stillwaters" for *Trout Tales,* a regional fly fishing newsletter.

The Intruder

If you've been fly fishing for a while, you know from experience to keep your mouth shut about certain things. You know, for example, not to reveal the location of your secret spots to another fisherman because he'll probably blab it to at least two other guys. They, in turn, will each tell two more, and so on until, before you can say "cutthroat," the number of fishermen tromping through your honey hole will have grown to about two zillion—plus or minus a horde or two. Consequently, you've learned to guard your fishing spots like a sow grizzly guards her cubs. When it comes to the secret places, you ain't tellin' nobody nuthin'. Mum's the word.

Okay, but let's suppose you drive back into old Rooster Poot Road one day to catch the yellow stonefly hatch on your favorite riffle, and there, horror of horrors, hidden in the trees, sits a shiny new SUV with out-of-state plates. Uh-oh, you think, word's finally leaked out.

Either that, or some idiot tourist has just bungled onto my spot.

Your heart sinks. You have half a mind to leave, but you know the Yellow Sallies are going to be boiling out of this riffle in an hour or two, and the brookies and cutts are gonna' be on 'em like sharks on a wounded tuna. You want to be there when it happens.

What's a guy to do? Well, you could leave, but then you'd likely spend the rest of the day whining about the %#@** tourist who drove you off your private water. And, of course, you'd miss the hatch. Nix that idea.

You could wade in alongside of him, play dumb, and hope he's not one of those certified black belt combat anglers you read about in the papers every now and then. You've seen this insidious bit of angling trickery employed with a fair amount of success on a couple of rivers in Montana.

You've seen it backfire too, with predictably nasty results. In any case, rudeness plays no part in your brand of fly fishing.

Besides, you're too light to fight, and too thin to win. Scratch that tactic.

You could sit on the bank and wait him out. That's acceptable on big, heavily fished rivers, but far too intrusive on small creeks and streams where half the reason for being there in the first place is to lose yourself in solitude. You wouldn't want anyone doing it to you.

You finally decide to surrender graciously, and just slink off downstream without disturbing the tourist. It stings a little, but you know it's the right thing to do, and there is another piece of water down the creek that's almost as good as this one. You're about to trudge off when you're suddenly overcome by what—a burst of compassion? Sympathy? Magnanimity? You don't know, but it occurs to you the guy's from out of state, probably doesn't have a clue about the Yellow Sallies, and what the hell, he's already in the water, isn't he? Maybe you should just tell him about the imminent hatch, and give him a couple of size 14 yellow soft hackles you know will drive the fish crazy once the bugs start coming off. What have you got to lose?

You whistle softly to get his attention, and in the course of the next few minutes fill him in on the hatch, the flies and the fish.

You tell him how they seem to prefer the soft hackle to the dry fly, how they take best on the downstream swing, and that the cutts will be lurking in the quieter water.

"They're Greenbacks," you tell him, "rare, wild, strikingly beautiful. Hardly anyone knows they're in here." You hope he picks up on that, and that he'll keep his mouth shut.

He thanks you profoundly for your help, and as you're about to leave asks if you'd like to stay and fish the hatch with him.

"Geez, that'd be great," you say. "Sure you don't mind? I don't want to intrude."

"Nonsense," he says. "There's plenty of room here, and besides, one good turn deserves another, doesn't it? By the way," he winks, "don't worry, I won't tell another soul about this place."

Right about then, a Yellow Sally helicopters by, wings sparkling in the morning sun. Upstream, your tourist buddy has a fish dancing at the end of his line. Looks like it's going to be a great day after all.

Dorothy Schramm
Pentwater, Michigan

Schramm owns Rodsmith, a custom rod and repair business. She is a FFF Certified Casting Instructor and had taught both for both Sage casting and Orvis Fly Fishing schools in the Midwest.

She is past President of Flygirls of Michigan, a FFF

women's fly fishing network; Director of the Anglers of the AuSable; member of Lew Jewett Fly Fishers, Red Cedar Fly Fishers, Brotherhood of the Jungle Cock, and West Michigan Hacklers; and Steering Committee member of the Pentwater River Watershed group.

From *The Flygirls Newsletter*
September, 1998

*E*very sport has its "rules of the road" or etiquette or just plain manners. All fly schools and guides should teach it and every book on fly fishing should include the subject. It is easy. Just treat others on the river as you would wish to be treated. Most people fly fish because they value solitude. Respect that idea. Good communication is the best tool we have to prevent misunderstandings or sour confrontations, and this includes canoeists, tubers, and other river users.

Recently, while fishing a popular Michigan river, I rounded a bend, working my way downstream at a steady pace, followed by another woman fairly new to the sport. A young man walked up the path across the river, dropped in about 15 yards below me and proceeded to fish downstream directly in front of me.

Having remained silent in such situations for the better part of twenty years on the water, I whistled to get his attention, then sarcastically asked, "Are you planning to jump in front of me and fish downstream?" I saw his enthusiasm melt and he stopped all movement waiting for what might come next. He said that he didn't know which way I was going.

I didn't want the opportunity for communication to deteriorate as I had already dealt a heavy blow and was feeling bad about it. I told him that I wish he had just asked and that my plan was to get out of the river, drop a long distance below him, and give him plenty of room to fish. He sincerely apologized and I suggested better communication in the future. All ended well but it could have started better.

Be prepared for such encounters and take the opportunity to help educate those who have never been taught the basic courtesies of the sport. In MY experience, I was unprepared for what to say and was disgusted with my sarcasm.

In the future when something like this happens, I will open the discussion with a question about flies or equipment and then make a suggestion about sharing the water. Perhaps sharing a few flies or some information would ease tensions. When I encounter someone already fishing, I usually state my intention. "I don't want to crowd you" or "Are you moving up or downstream?" are good openers and help to diffuse a potential confrontation.

While eager to treat others well, I was not prepared when I was on the receiving end of bad manners. Along with working on my presentation of my fly, I think I'll work on my presentation of manners.

Avoid crowds: Act weird.

JACK GARTSIDE
Boston, Massachusetts

A world-famous tier and angler, someone once said of him, "Jack was never one to let convention get in his way." That's putting it mildly.

He was seen one week camping under the stars on the beaches of the Yucatan, fishing the bocas late into the night; and the next week, he was successfully pursuing stripers in Boston Harbor riding Gerald, his rubber giraffe. One more solution to avoiding crowds: People avoid Gartside because he looks rather odd fishing from a rubber giraffe.

He gave up a career as an English teacher to become a Boston cabby, thus enabling himself to have more time to pursue his passion for fly fishing and for tying his exquisite fly patterns.

Somehow, it does not come as a surprise that Jack Gartside would have a rather original philosophy and

approach to fly fishing etiquette, which he expresses in
the following letter to the author:

Sept.7, 1997

Dear Rhea,

Your book on etiquette sounds interesting. I'm not
sure what (or whether) I could contribute to it,
however, as I almost *never* fish in a situation
where etiquette would be required. To me, two is
a crowd and I much prefer to fish alone. This
summer, in fact, I've not run into even a single
fisherman in the waters that I fish. This is by
design and not happenstance.

If you come up this way, give me a buzz, and perhaps we can fish together. I should warn you, however, that it's all wading and walking and covering
lots of water. Typically I'll walk several miles
through water to cover a flat or stretch of shoreline.
It's not for the faint-hearted or for those who
expect success to come easily. But that's not you.
Just thought I'd mention it *by way of preparation—a
form of etiquette too,* you might say. I simply avoid
the "popular" places. And the beat goes on . . .

So, I do not know what I could add to your book,
except the following thought:

The best etiquette is to avoid etiquette.

All the best,

Jack

———∞∞∞———

DICK TALLEUR
Manchester, New Hampshire

An avid angler since childhood, Dick Talleur's angling passion has taken him from Alaska's trout and salmon wonderland, to Iceland's geysers and glaciers, to England's legendary chalk streams, to Russia's Kola Peninsula, and to Montana, which has become a sort of second home. Dick teaches fly tying and fishing all over the USA, Canada, England, Scandinavia, and in Russia, where he manages two salmon-fishing programs.

Dick is a prolific and important contributor to angling literature, having authored several successful books such as *Mastering The Art Of Fly Tying*, *The Fly-Tyer's Primer*, *Fly Fishing for Trout*, *The Versatile Fly Tyer*, *Talleur's Dry Fly Handbook*, *Modern Fly-Tying Materials*, *The L. L. Bean Fly Tying Handbook*, *Pretty And Practical Salmon Flies*, *Guide To Fly Tying*, and *Mastering The Art Of Fly Tying*. He has produced fourteen videos on fly tying with Jim and Kelly Watt of *Flyfishing Video* magazine.

From *Fly Fishing for Trout*
Winchester Press, 1974

*T*he trout seemed in no great distress as he moved upstream at a moderate pace and then rolled on the surface and reversed direction. For an instant a broad flank was revealed and I realized that this fish was larger than I had guessed, perhaps a twenty-incher, maybe even more. My heart began to pound audibly.

I girded for a long struggle, but it was not to be. As the fish determinedly bore downstream I saw a stump on the water's edge, with exposed roots visible beneath the undercut bank. Immediately I perceived his purpose and, seeking to turn him, I applied as much pressure as 6x can bear, perhaps a bit more. Whether or not my antagonist reached the roots, I will never know; suffice to say that, with a jarring snap, he was free.

As I reeled in, there was disappointment, but it was tempered with an overriding sense of exhilaration. I had risen a great trout on one of the most challenging stretches of water in the country, and he might well be there for another encounter one day.

I replaced my fly not without some difficulty, because my hands were trembling and I was about to begin a false cast when I heard a distinct sloshing. Glancing over my shoulder, I was consternated to see the lone fisherman charging up the pool, smiling a greeting: "Hi, mind if I help you catch those trout? Things are dead below." I gesticulated wildly, pleading for him to halt in his tracks, but by the time he comprehended, the damage was done. Waves rippled across the water, lapped against the shore, and all rises ceased abruptly.

With an effort, I held my temper, as I realized this crestfallen fellow had no premonition of what had transpired. Across twenty feet of water we became acquainted, as I elaborated on the problems posed by the calm, flat pool. As comprehension dawned, he became sincerely apologetic.

Sympathetic, I outfitted my new acquaintance with some 6x tippet material and a few size 16 Red Quills. This is one of the beauties of being a flytier: one can afford to be magnanimous, which is a kick in itself. We then separated, wading carefully until there was perhaps fifty feet between us, whereupon we began our vigil.

DAVE WHITLOCK
Midway, Arkansas

Twenty-five years ago, Whitlock resigned his job as a research chemist to become a full-time fly fishing professional. He now lives near the White River in northwest Arkansas, where he and his wife, Emily, operate the Whitlock Fly Fishing School.

His talents include painting, illustrating, writing, and photography. Whitlock wrote and illustrated the *L.L. Bean Fly-Fishing Handbook*, the *L.L. Bean Fly Fishing for Bass Handbook*, *Imitating and Fishing Natural Fish Foods*, and his *Guide to Aquatic Trout Foods*.

Perhaps his most notable contribution to wild trout is

the Whitlock-Vibert Box, an in-stream salmonoid egg incubator.

Fly Fishing: Today and Tomorrow

I've heard many folks say lately that they feel that fly fishing is becoming so popular it is in danger of being *loved to death*. I've always wanted to see more people do at least some part of their fishing with a fly rod. It can be such a peaceful, poetic sport that seems to help renew our spirits—and we all need more of that these days to help us live more peaceful lives. At the same time though, I worry about the overcrowding and overuse of some of our beautiful, classic trout fishing destinations.

Fly fishing is such a great sport that it is truly unfair for us to say "OK, now that I'm a fly fisher, there are enough of us and no one else should take it up." We are not going to stop, nor should we, the progressive promotion of fly fishing. Besides, our rivers and fish really do need all the friends they can get, and a thoughtful, caring and educated fly fisher can be a true caretaker of these resources. Also, a large body of fly fishers can make a real difference in influencing laws that protect our environment, especially since they are actually *out in* the environment and can see and act as problems come up.

What we can do is make our impact on the resources more acceptable, and this is where I see the real problem with some of the "new generation" of fly fishers, because there seems to be a lot of rude and inconsiderate behavior showing up on the streams these days. This is something that has not been very common in the past, and on ever more crowded waters, etiquette and courtesy become very important.

For example: Recently, on a catch and release section of my

home water, the White River in Arkansas, I fished with five other friends. We had a wonderful day sharing the water with no problems. Then, about a week later, I was back on the same 100 yard stretch, alone—until three unknown fly fishers approached the area. They were loud, careless, used vulgar language, tossed cigarette butts in the water, and waded through my run, putting down every trout around. What was the difference in these three spoilers and the six of us the week before who had fished together so pleasantly?

I believe it was a matter of understanding and using good stream etiquette. It seems as though there is a marked lack of mentors these days. My parents and grandparents were all anglers, and wonderful role models. They taught me not only how to catch fish, but also how to respect fish, other anglers, and the outdoors. The longer I live, the more I realize how fortunate I was to have such good early guidance. Today many new anglers must learn about outdoor behavior and respect from other anglers or teachers. In the past (and for many still today), most of us were educated in good sportsmanship by a parent or grandparent, scout master, fly fishing friend, fly shop or organization, or with help from books and articles that stressed sportsmanship. We were usually taught at least the Golden Rule of sportsmanship (and life for that matter): "Treat others as you would like them to treat you." Because of this, we were generally very conscious of our impact on other folks, the peacefulness and the fish in the waters. This is one of the areas that seems to be missing in the educational process of some of the fishers on many lakes and streams now, and it diminishes the quality of the fly fishing experience for all of us.

I believe that many of the problems that are now occurring in the crowded fly fishing areas could be lessened greatly if each of us is determined to be a good example and try to teach all those we can the principles of the Golden Rule.

One of the nicest common veins fly fishers seem to share is an unselfish attitude toward other fly fishers, especially those needing help with tackle, flies, casting, or techniques. I have always been proud of us for being that way. Be sure to take advantage of it now; and later, when you are thus skilled, help those who are as you were once yourself.

Because a lot of serious anglers have worked hard to protect our waters, the future of fly fishing is bright today. But, you will have to help if it is to remain so. Keep improving your skills; keep trying to catch more species of fish on the fly; help protect our fisheries—and have lots of fun fly fishing.

To conclude, we should welcome new, enthusiastic fly fishers and then help each one learn the fly fishing etiquette and ethics that have been passed down for so many years and that have helped this sport be so resource-conscious and so wonderfully enjoyable.

CATHY AND BARRY BECK

Benton, Pennsylvania

Cathy and Barry Beck live in the Fishing Creek Valley of northeastern Pennsylvania. They host fly fishing trips to exotic fresh- and saltwater destinations for Frontiers Travel, as well as conduct fly fishing schools and clinics and give presentations. As noted photographers, their work appears regularly on sporting calendars and in fishing magazines.

Their books include Cathy Beck's *Fly Fishing Handbook*, an all-inclusive guide to fly fishing; *Seasons of the Bighorn*, a collaborative photographic journal; and *From Fresh to Salt*, a handbook and guide for the saltwater fly fisherman.

Situations Vary Tremendously

*F*ishing etiquette is somewhat difficult to write about. Because it is such a varied subject, it changes geographically, and what becomes totally acceptable in one area might be considered extremely rude in another.

Take, for instance, trout fishing. On the Yellow Breeches in Boiling Springs, Pennsylvania, anglers often fish close enough to cast over each other's lines. And sometimes do, much to the chagrin of others. The Yellow Breeches is a very popular place to fish. It's easy for a lot of people to get to, it's a small stream, it offers good fishing, and it is well known. Any of these reasons alone would be enough to make it crowded.

We once saw a fisherman lose his spot when he stepped out to put on his jacket, which was lying on the stream bank directly behind him. When he turned around to walk back in someone had taken his place.

On the other hand, visit the same size stream in almost any other area, and other rules apply. Most fly fishermen like their own space. It's part of the appeal: communing with nature on a personal level. We like it when we're alone on the water, when we can comfortably move up or downstream as we please without fishing in someone else's pocket.

Inexperienced fly fishermen are often unsure of what is considered an appropriate distance from other fishermen. There are a couple of things to take into consideration here. First of all, if you get to the stream and find another fisherman already fishing, just be content to observe for a few minutes. Watch to see if they are working their way downstream or upstream and, when you do enter, always enter into water they've already fished. It's very rude to have someone walk into water you're about to fish.

If it's a small stream and you're close enough to talk to the other fishermen, it's polite to ask if they mind if you fish well behind them. Almost any fisherman will welcome you if you don't crowd or push. After all, it may be your favorite pool and maybe your only day off to fish, but they still got there first, and maybe it's their favorite pool and only day too.

When you do enter, wade quietly and slowly so that you don't scare any of the fish. Mind your own business, keep to yourself, (that means keep quiet) and everything should go well for both of you.

If you happen to be the other fisherman, and someone shows up to fish the same pool, be polite. This may be a new fisherman and sometimes what we take for rudeness is just ignorance. The only way to learn is to be taught, and sometimes, by calmly explaining when something is wrong, we're helping to teach. Getting mad and telling him off or stomping out of the water is only going to ruin our day. So, if another fisherman moves in without asking to fish the same pool or run, explain that you're fishing up or down, and suggest that he may get in where you've already fished.

There is no way to prevent all misunderstandings or encounters that leave us annoyed or mad. It will help if we assume that the other person may not know any better, instead of thinking that he's an obnoxious *@%*.

Different conditions apply when sharing a boat with a fishing partner. It's usually a bit tight to have two fishermen fly fishing out of the boat at the same time. If you fish with each other often and there are just two of you in the boat, you may be able to work out a system that works smoothly.

Otherwise, it's probably best to take turns, especially if you're with a third person, the guide. Most fishermen, when fishing saltwater flats with a guide, will take half-hour turns. This gives both fishermen the same amount of fishing time.

Of course, if you're up for half an hour and don't see anything and your partner gets up and catches three fish right off the bat, you may have to remind yourself that it's still his half-hour. On the other hand, he may feel generous and invite you to fish on his time. But, it's his call completely. And, who knows, the next half-hour may be hot for you and the same courtesy should be returned.

It can be frustrating when one fisherman is more experienced than the other. If a good fisherman gets up and catches fish whenever the opportunity comes along, and the other fisherman gets up and can't make the cast in time or stands on the line, or fumbles it and spooks the fish, it may become very frustrating for everyone in the boat. We've seen great friendships develop by sharing a boat, and we've seen them disintegrate very quickly.

There are ways to help each other in a boat too. The person sitting can make sure that the line on the deck stays clear and untangled. If the angler needs to switch rods, the partner can take the rod not being fished and hand over the other one. While the angler is getting ready to cast the new rod, the partner can be reeling in the first rod and getting it out of the way. This happens often when there are bonefish and permit on the same flat and different rods are required. The switch has to be made very quickly.

Sharing fishing time and space is often necessary and it can be a pleasant experience. It all goes back to treating others as you would like to be treated. Most of the time things go smoothly. Very rarely do we run into a fisherman who is so irritating that there's just no hope. When it happens, we just move and get away from him. In general, fly fishermen are very nice people and most are thoughtful and polite.

If we all treat each other as we would like to be treated, everyone would have a more pleasant experience on the stream.

And, by setting the example and leading the way, we may be helping the next generation of fishermen to be kind and thoughtful.

MALLORY BURTON
Prince Rupert, British Columbia, Canada

Mallory Burton is the daughter of a Canadian hockey player and fishing guide. She lives in Prince Rupert, B.C., but her heart belongs to Montana. Her essays and fiction have appeared in numerous anthologies and fly fishing trade magazines. She fishes for steelhead, trout, and salmon in the winter months, and spends her summers fishing for trout.

Messing With the River Gods

From *Reading the Waters: Stories and Essays of Fly Fishing and Life,*
Keokee Press, 1995

*E*very season for the past 10 seasons, you have made a faithful pilgrimage to this river of rivers. In all the years you have visited these waters, you have taken away with you only the memories of a few special fish. You have left behind only your footprints and perhaps a few flies in the willows. In the company of other anglers, you have referred to this stretch of water only as the River X.

You figure your fishing karma on this particular river must be pretty good. So why in the name of all the river gods is the 10 o'clock *trico* hatch in full swing at 9:30 in the morning? And why is another fisherman standing in the middle of your favorite run with a good fish bending his rod and better fish rising all around him?

Under these circumstances, a lesser angler might rudely cut in upstream and muddy up the bottom of the river real good. But not you. Fortunately, or unfortunately depending on how you look at it, your fishing manners are impeccable. You'd no more cut in upstream than go fishing with a can of worms and a jar of cheese balls. It's not that you're a fanatic about stream etiquette. It's just that it doesn't pay to mess with the river gods.

You step into the water at a respectful distance downstream and watch as the gentleman lands his fish. He raises the net revealing the big forked tail and grayish mottled sides of what is obviously the most disgusting whitefish in three counties. A smile creeps over your face. Slowly everything begins to make perfect sense. After all, if the river gods have seen fit to place another angler in your favorite fishing spot and transform that spot into whitefish heaven, who are you to question their motives? Trusting entirely in their wisdom, you tie on a size 20 *trico* and calmly shake out a few feet of line.

Something catches your eye on the bottom of the stream. Through the swirling water, you can clearly make out a huge red-orange lure, all three of its barbaric hooks grinning up at you. Your forehead wrinkles in disgust. The river gods will not be pleased. You feel it is somehow your duty to remove the offending object from their domain. On the other hand, the water is waist-deep and spring-creek cold. You'll take a bath if you reach for it.

Just then, a few feet off the right riverbank, something very curious happens which suddenly demands your full attention. In smooth, flat water, all of six inches deep, a small boulder suddenly appears and behind it, a riffle that fans out four feet wide and 20 feet long. As you watch, the boulder disappears, reappears, and eats a *trico*. You dare to hope that the riffle is, in fact, a raft of feeding fish lying tail-to-snout in the wake of the monster at their head.

You fire a perfect cast at the head fish, cursing your stupidity the instant the fly hits the water. If you hook or even spook the lead fish, the others will scatter. You hold your mouth just right, and the fish ignores your fly. The fish behind him goes for it and misses. The fly slides over the back of another fish and into the upper jaw of the next fish down the line. You set the hook and the fish comes obediently downstream, silvery-pink sides flashing.

You decide to pick off the trout one by one, working through the 14-inchers at the back toward the monster at the front. You cast into the tail-end of the pack. A fish turns and pursues the fly downstream, nearly colliding with another fish that streaks over to snatch it away. You land this fish, another saucy rainbow, and release him.

Then it happens. The upstream fisherman reels in, clambers up the bank, and starts walking towards you. He takes his time, stopping every few feet to peer over the side of the undercut right riverbank. Panic-stricken, you gesture frantically, motioning the intruder away from the bank, away from your fish. The angler stops in his tracks, looking puzzled. Then he turns in the direction of your frenzied pointing and nods his head, finally comprehending.

"Grouse," he shouts, cupping his hands around his mouth so that the sound will carry even better. "A pair." And he keeps on coming.

For centuries, the rules of fishing etiquette have been modeled by esteemed mentors and publicized by concerned writers. Trouble is, there exists no effective means of enforcing them. If an angler chooses to walk downstream close to the bank, shouting, there is nothing to prevent him or her from doing so.

You find yourself wishing that every fishing vest came equipped with a hand grenade. No, not a hand grenade. That would be too noisy. What you really need is a bow and a single silent arrow, straight and true. Thwack. Toppling the intruder backwards. Away from the fish. You wonder whether the jurisdiction of the river gods extends above the high-water mark.

The riffle disappears, dark shapes streaking past you on every side and with them your dark thoughts. The madness passes, and the gentle angler within you returns to inhabit your waders. You remind yourself that the creature on the bank is a human being, while the creatures in the water are, after all, only stupid fish.

"Howdy," says the human being, smiling and oblivious.

"Catchinany?"

"A few," you say. "But it looks like it's all over now."

"What about later?" he asks. "Boys at the shop said this river's got a noon hatch of mayflies."

You nod in agreement. "Some stretches are better than others," you say thoughtfully. "There's a decent stretch about four miles upstream. Turnoff is just after the bridge. Can't miss it."

The two of you hike back to where your cars are parked, chatting amiably. You take down your rod and offer him a beer. You give him a half-dozen of the sparkle duns you tied in the wee hours of last night.

"What do I owe you for the flies?" he asks.

"Tell you what," you say. "The next time you're on your home river, just give away a few flies, and we'll call it even."

"I'll do that," he says. "People sure are friendly around here."

As his pickup heads off down the road, you give him the thumbs up sign. Then you string up your rod again, faster than you thought humanly possible. On the way back down the trail, you make a bargain with the river gods. If they bring back the riffle fish, you will take a swim in the icy river to retrieve the treble-hooked lure that is currently polluting their aquatic environment.

The river gods keep their end of the bargain. By the time you have hiked back down the trail, mayflies are popping all over the place, and the fish are back. You take 20 fish in 20 casts. The big rainbow goes four pounds easy.

You forget about your end of the bargain. Understandably, when you're having a day like the one you're having, you tend to get a little preoccupied. As you release the big trout and watch him swim away, you feel positively light-headed. You take a few steps toward the bank and trip over a boulder you're sure wasn't there this morning. As you go under, sputtering, you remember the lure. You mark its location with the toe of your boot, take a deep breath, and plunge into the icy water again and again. It's not that you're a fanatic about stream garbage. It's just that it doesn't pay to mess with the river gods.

AL KYTE
Moraga, California

In 1994, Al Kyte gave a questionnaire to fifty California fly fishers. It was composed of twelve etiquette scenarios. He offered choices for solutions, as well as space for comments. From this, he organized his findings into these seven principles or "points of etiquette." All of them were beyond the easy issues of closing gates behind one's car, slowing down in dusty parking areas, and taking care not to litter.

In Search Of Etiquette
From *California Fly Fisher*, September 1994

I turned my back to let my gaze follow the creek's cascading descent, but then stopped short. My eyes had caught a movement in the distance—the back-and-forth glint of a waving fly rod. An angler, the first I had encountered on the creek that year, was working my way. Hurriedly, I stuffed the remainder of my sandwich into the creel and drew back into the alders. I needed to put more streams between us. It was 1946, and the only fishing etiquette I understood was that any visible angler was too close.

Nearly a half a century later, angling solitude is likely to be broken in minutes rather than days. On well-known waters, a traffic cop, rather than a game warden, seems more fitting. Even people new to the sport can share a horror story of some angler's deplorable manners. In short, the worst of today's highway behavior has been spilling over into the trout stream.

When I think of etiquette, the focus shifts from myself to my interactions with other people. Etiquette is synonymous with a social code, rules of conduct, and manners. It is the standard of what is socially acceptable in conduct as prescribed by authority or convention. Ultimately, it involves making a choice that honors another's rights as much as my own. Often today The Golden Rule seems to give way to another code: "Looking Out for Number One."

Etiquette is not that simple due to the fact that accepted guidelines vary with the waters and tactics one fishes; the acceptable spacing on a large river, for example, often constitutes crowding on a small stream.

1. **"First come, first served" establishes basic right-of-way.**
Unanimously it was agreed to the above, and that other
anglers are obliged to go elsewhere or wait for the first angler
to move on. The acceptance of this principle is what motivates people to arrive early and sometimes, in an unattractive
spectacle, literally race one another to the water. This principle also gives the stationary angler the right-of-way over a
moving angler, such as one fishing from a drift boat.

   This right carries no time limit, despite the tendency to
be critical when someone "hogs" the best water. The spirit
of etiquette might be expressed by the angler who leaves a
prime spot to others after a reasonable time period. This,
sadly, does not happen often.

   One common situation occurs on small streams when
two anglers fish toward each other. Each is disturbing the
water the other would fish next, and one should stop and
relinquish the remaining water to the other. Long-
standing tradition favors the upstream-fishing angle, yet
many novices today seem unaware of this tradition. It often
is like playing a stream version of "Chicken."

2. **Anglers should allow for critical access routes to other
water.** As people converge in ever-increasing numbers on
favorite fishing spots, one needs to recognize places where
an angler's fishing interferes with another's ability to access
the water. The water adjacent to the Buffalo Ford parking
lot on the Yellowstone is a case in point. Unless the river is
low, there is only one safe place for a wader to cross over to
access the far side. Problems occur when people start
casting in water that must be waded through. I believe that
key access areas should be posted to communicate right-
of-way for the angler passing through.

3. **Casting into an occupied pool generally constitutes crowding.** Crowding is perhaps the most common breach of fishing etiquette. The distance between two anglers varies with the size of the river, the character of adjacent pools, the quality of the fishing, and how well you know the other people.

   How much fishing water should be relinquished when bypassing another angler? The general consensus here is that one could either commence fishing when out of view, or after leaving a half hour of undisturbed water.

   What if you move up to an angler who is fishing one of your favorite runs from the opposite side of the river? Some feel it acceptable to fish the water tight to the bank if beyond the reach of the other angler. But the majority feel one should not cast into the pool being fished. They would wait to fish it or return later in the day.

4. **Casting to someone else's risers or standing in the way of that person's cast or drift lane constitutes crowding.** The "occupied pool" principle serves as a standard on rivers with distinct pools and runs, but what defines crowding on smooth surfaces of spring creeks or lakes?

   Perhaps the best visible guideline here is the cast of the first angler. I've seen float tubers mark their territory by fanning long casts toward an approaching angler in a non-verbal message of the amount of water they are covering.

   Andre Puyans says, "Move only close enough to communicate and observe, but never close enough to interfere." Some suggest the "two or three cast" guideline, leaving a little unfished water between one cast and someone else's.

5. **Crowding is related to an angler's rate of movement.** People new to the sport often underestimate how rapidly

anglers can move along a creek. Small narrow pools are quickly fished, and an energetic angler might cover several miles during a day's fishing. Streamside foliage often forces the angler to wade up a creek, disturbing a high percentage of fish. I recall more than a few days when a surprising lack of rising fish was eventually explained by the discovery of someone wading upstream 15 to 20 minutes ahead of me.

How much water should one give up after over-taking an upstream angler? Three-fourths of the group agreed that they would either observe the angler's rate of movement and then walk upstream far enough to relinquish half an hour of undisturbed water or, walk far enough upstream that they aren't likely to see that angler again. Cutting in too close invites an angling version of "leap frog," in which two anglers pass one another throughout the day. Each one spends too much fishing time walking around the other. However, this can be fun for friends who enjoy fishing together.

If someone cuts me off on a small stream, I have learned to by-pass them, check my watch, and force myself to walk for full 20 minutes before fishing again.

6. **Movement along streams can spook fish.** It is possible to interfere with someone's fishing without casting a fly. If I allow my dog to splash in the water nearby, my children to throw rocks, or someone in my party to talk loudly or play loud music I disturb both the angler and the fish. It is important to find a route well back from the bank to avoid spooking fish, and even farther back around any angler in the water.

Boat anglers, when passing others, need to consider slowing down as much as possible, sitting down to present a low profile, attempt to avoid creating unnecessary noise from anchors, motors, or oars. The boater might ask the wading angler which side to pass on. Fly fishers sometimes err in underestimating how far a spin fisherman can cast and cover water.

7. **Courteous communications can defuse conflicts.** This is perhaps the real key to addressing etiquette problems. There are benefits in communicating on the stream, even for those who savor solitude. An angler whose body language or tone is unfriendly can always be left alone.

What about resting a fish when another angler approaches with the intent to fish the same spot? Because so many anglers today don't know the protocol, it is wise to initiate a conversation to inform the approaching angler of your plans. And, as you arrived there first, you do have priority.

Distinctive local customs might be communicated as well. For example, the steelhead lineup and rotation is a local custom that might raise avoidable conflicts. However, steelhead guides see their share of ugly confrontations and recognize limitations to the courteous communications approach. The "lineup" has a social code that is most vehemently enforced. When first in from the ocean, steelhead remain tightly grouped. Thus competition to put one's fly in the bucket is extreme. Anglers often stand as close to one another as possible without risking injury. Many people have stopped fishing in lineups because of the unpleasantness. If an angler leaves the lineup to answer the call of Nature, they should not expect to get back into the same spot unless next to friends. Typically, only if you move out of the lineup to play a fish might you expect to return to your spot.

More impressive than the answers to my census was the overall level of concern expressed about the growing etiquette problem. Virtually every person in the study agreed that breaches of angling courtesy have become far too common. I believe Ernie Schwiebert hit the nail on the head in stating, "Stream etiquette in the past was always carefully taught to each succeeding generation, but such tutelage has too often been lost in the explosive growth of fly fishing."

Many leaders in our sport have succeeded in promoting their teaching and fishing skills, as well as the conservation practice of catch-and-release fishing. It is time to put forth this same concerted emphasis into the communication of angling etiquette.

I believe that anyone who teaches a fly-fishing class, certifies casting instructors, operates a shop, is involved in a club, and produces publications has the obligation to communicate the important principles of angling courtesy. Sessions on etiquette need to be included as programs. I would like to think that leaders in this sport could influence an improvement in manners, thus avoiding the necessity for posting regulations regarding fishing behavior.

As Oregon guide John Judy puts it, "The competition to be first is sometimes pretty ugly; it brings out the worst in fishermen."

John Sullivan, now with the California Department of Fish and Game, compared fishing etiquette to the ways people drive a car. "On city streets and highways, one takes account of the car, not the person inside. But on many small back roads, total strangers driving toward one another will signal a hello as they pass—sometimes just a friendly subtle lifting of the fingers from the wheel. The same kind of general recognition of one another on trout waters can be a first step in the search for etiquette—and make for a happier fishing experience all the way around."

And so, as I continue to pick my way along trout waters, I believe I will make a greater use of a smile, nod, and even a brief chat. I will continue to give others the space I would like them to give me. If I observe a breach of etiquette, I will try to offer advice in as friendly a manner as possible. I will make an effort to see my fellow angler as a friend I haven't met, rather than as a rival for the same fish.

MIKE LAWSON
Island Park, Idaho

Former owner of Henry's Fork Anglers, Inc., Mike Lawson has seen a lot of changes and an increase in fishing pressure on his famed waters, and has some strong opinions on what needs to be done.

He is a sought-after lecturer and presents slide shows and casting and fly tying demos. He still gives a few fly fishing schools, in which he always includes time to cover streamside behavior. His most recent book is *Spring Creeks*.

Some Thoughts on Etiquette

$\mathcal{M}$any anglers believe that the best fishing is found in remote areas that the general public hasn't discovered. That was often true in the good old days. Growing up in southeastern Idaho, I knew plenty of places where I could walk a mile or so and find plenty of solitude and large trout. Today, even if you hike five or six miles, you're likely to find other anglers sharing your favorite water. Even in remote Alaska, fishermen crowd the most productive waters. The challenge we face today is to experience the pleasantries of trout fishing without infringing on the experience of others.

The rules of stream etiquette are hard to define, and they vary from stream to stream. Anglers accustomed to fishing elbow to elbow in one of Missouri's best known state parks have a different set of rules than those who fish the waters of the sparsely populated Rocky Mountains. When you visit a new area, you need to learn the basic rules of etiquette for the local water.

A good friend of mine told me about an experience he had on the San Juan River in New Mexico. On his first day there, he arrived early in the morning, staked out a good stretch of water, and landed a couple of good trout. After he tied on a new fly he looked up and saw that another angler had moved into the same pool only a few yards away. He gave the intruder a hard stare, to avoid a confrontation, reeled up and left. As the day progressed and the river became more crowded, he noticed that there were plenty of anglers who seemed to be casting into each other's waders. He realized that if he wanted to enjoy the fabulous fishing on the San Juan, he'd have to adjust to the rules of the river and share. With that in mind, he decided to give it another try. He caught several more good trout and made some new friends in the process. But he decided that such crowded conditions weren't for him and he has never returned.

Almost every angler has had a feeding fish they are working put down by a clumsy angler walking or wading too close. Usually, these anglers don't know any better. They don't know the specifics of acceptable behavior. The Henry's Fork is famous for its big bank feeders. When you see an angler fishing against the bank you should give the angler and the fish plenty of room. You should go out of your way to accommodate the situation. If an unknowing angler walks too close and spooks a fish you are working, be ready for them to ask, "How's the fishing?" Of course, the temptation is to say, "Very good until you showed up." But the best response is to keep quiet and look for another fish. If you can put your anger behind you, it might be possible to tactfully explain the situation to the offending angler and save him further embarrassment in the future.

I've seen some terrible things happen because of poor on stream manners. Verbal and even physical conflicts result in a negative experience for everyone. There will always be a few jerks who act like they own the river and don't care what anybody thinks, but I believe most anglers want to do the right thing. Their most important concern is to enjoy the experience and not infringe on the experience of others.

Noise can be extremely annoying. Most of us fish for reasons other than catching fish. I personally get special satisfaction from the quietness of a soft flowing trout stream. I like to hear the birds singing, the breeze thru the willows, and most of all, the slurp of a large feeding trout. I fish to escape the noise pollution so common in everyday life. The last thing I want to hear is hollering and shouting. It is natural to get excited over hooking a large fish, and some anglers scream and yell to celebrate such an event. These antics should be kept to a minimum out of respect for the place and the other anglers sharing it.

Conflicts with boating and wading anglers are common on most western waters. I remember when I was fishing the Missouri River and a boat almost drowned me. I was in up to the top of my waders trying to cast to a big rising trout near the middle of the river when I looked upstream and saw a boat bearing down on me. I waved my arms and shouted. When I realized the oarsman wasn't going to change course, I tried to wade to safety and almost didn't make it. My waders filled with water and I ended up swimming for my life.

If you are in a boat, you need to be careful not to infringe upon other anglers' space. Remember, the water restricts wading anglers to a specific stretch of water. You can go anywhere if you are in a boat. Make sure to give wade waders plenty of room and, if possible, row to the other side of the stream to pass them.

On smaller waters you may have to float through someone else's fishing water to get past. Be sure to reel up so as not to cast into their water as you drift through. Most anglers who wade these smaller waters understand the code of behavior for float boaters. The Beaverhead in Montana is frequently crowded as waders fish the best runs and floaters drift from one run to the next. It always amazes me how everyone seems to get along on this crowded river. It is also surprising how quickly trout start rising again after a boat passes over them. Fish simply adjust to the boats.

If you are wade fishing and you see a boat approaching, make sure to give the floaters a good idea of the water you are fishing. When I approach a wading angler in my boat and see that he is casting to the bank, I try to drift behind him so I won't disturb his water. If I am already committed to one side and the angler turns and starts casting to the center, I have no choice but to float through his water.

On large rivers, where wade fishing is limited, boaters should be even more considerate. If the river is crowded, you should leave easy to reach riffles and runs alone, even if no one is fishing them.

When I got into the outfitting business over twenty years ago, guides did almost all of the float boating. Now guides are in the minority on most waters. Unfortunately, there is still a perception that most float boaters are guides—and guides get blamed for a lot of bad behavior. I believe that most guides are considerate and understanding. On all the rivers in Idaho, and on many others in the country, the state requires guides to have the name of their business posted on their boats. If you have a bad experience with a guide you should contact his outfitter and the appropriate licensing authorities.

We always try to encourage our guides to provide some instruction to their clients regarding etiquette. Since we have a shop and a guide service I try to impress on my guides that all of the anglers on the river are our customers. I don't ever want to hear a complaint about guides from other anglers. It still happens once in awhile, but not often.

The regulations on most of our best waters require us to release most or all of the trout we catch. The trout don't really belong to us, they belong to the river. Wild trout are not only better game than their hatchery counterparts, they fight harder, live longer, grow larger, and are more beautiful. They are also more important to the environment we share. Bald eagles, osprey, river otters and other predators are a welcome addition to my fishing, and their survival depends on a healthy wild trout population. To watch an osprey dive with a mighty splash and rise up with a trout in his talons can be the highlight of an entire day of fishing.

Unfortunately, over the years I have seen some reckless attempts at releasing trout. Properly releasing a trout unharmed begins when you hook the fish. Stress and fatigue increase the longer you fight a fish. It may seem impressive to land a fish on a super-fine tippet but you should use the strongest tippet possible and land your fish quickly. Use the rod to fight the fish, always applying pressure opposite the direction the fish is moving. You can usually disorient a big fish and land him quickly without tiring him out completely. I believe a landing net with a soft-mesh bag is essential to landing a large fish without harm. Once in the net, keep the fish under water while removing the hook. Barbless hooks can be removed easily and help limit the handling of the fish. If you want a "hero picture," get the camera ready before lifting the fish from the water. Don't drag the fish out on the bank or on the deck of a boat. Remember, the fish you catch also belong to other anglers.

Finally, I think we need to consider limiting our catch. How many big fish is enough for one day? A local outfitter publishes a newspaper full of photos of big trout and stories of 75 to 100 fish days. Again, how many are enough? Proper fly fishing ethics must start with our attitudes.

I was lucky enough to grow up fishing the great trout waters of southeastern Idaho with my father and grandfather. They not only taught me the skills to catch fish, but also helped me understand how to enjoy them. They helped me realize that it isn't how many you catch, but how you catch them. I learned to enjoy fishing for the experience and not the result. Even when the limits were liberal enough to fill our freezer with trout, we never kept more than we needed.

Today, I don't believe that fishing is a right. Like hunting, it is a privilege. In spite of all of our efforts to carefully release fish unharmed, some of them will die. In other words, the more fish you catch the more fish you will kill. Anglers who keep score, counting every fish, should take up a sport where the score counts, like golf. Today, there is no place in fishing for such an attitude. I remember an old slogan that was popular when catch and release was just becoming fashionable:

"Limit your kill, don't kill your limit."

Today the slogan should simply say, "Limit your catch." If you are lucky enough to hit one of those special days when you just can't keep the fish off your hook, take a break. Relax. Enjoy the river and the scenery. Save a few fish for the next angler. Knowing that you could have caught more than you did will set you apart from everybody else. That's when you know you have arrived.

GARY GRANT
FFF President

Goals, Codes, and Rules of the Rod

*T*he Code of the Federation of Fly Fishers expresses the belief that ethical behavior is a key component of the angling experience, and that anglers must behave ethically towards each other, non-anglers, and the environment. Ethical angling behavior is not a destination for one to boast about reaching. Rather, it is a continuous journey that will improve the overall angling experience.

Federation of Fly Fishers Code of Angling Ethics
Copyright © 2002 by the Federation of Fly Fishers, Inc.

*T*he mission of the Federation of Fly Fishers is to lead activities that enhance and support the fly fishing experience for all anglers who fish with the artificial fly. As part of our efforts to educate through fly fishing, we believe that ethical behavior is a key component of the angling experience. While the need to preserve for all anglers the natural beauty and quality of fisheries for future generations is paramount, consideration for fellow anglers cannot be overlooked.

FFF believes it essential that fly anglers in all waters embrace an ethic that embodies consideration for the environment and for others whether they are fishing or not. This Code of Angling Ethics complements the Catch and Release philosophy that is the hallmark of the Federation of Fly Fishers and reflects the importance of ethical behavior for all anglers. Moreover, it provides a framework for improving the angling experience by combining consideration of the fishery with respectful conduct towards fellow anglers. Overall, the policy denotes a journey in ethical behavior for fly anglers and not a destination.

Person-to-person and person-to-resource ethics go hand-in-hand. Fly anglers strive to understand and practice the land ethic of Aldo Leopold, which extends ethical consideration to the land, plants, animals, fish, and water that comprise the entire ecosystem. An important part of this land ethic is that fly anglers support those programs that sustain high species diversity, and do not support policies that could cause the premature extinction of another species. The Native Fish Policy of the Federation of Fly Fishers is based on this ethic of preventing fish species extinction.

The following nine behaviors comprise the Federation of Fly Fishers Code of Angling Ethics:

- Angling ethics begin with understanding and obeying laws and regulations associated with the fishery. Fly anglers understand that their conduct relative to laws and regulations reflects on all anglers. Angling ethics begin with and transcend laws and regulations governing angling and the resources that sustain the sport.
- The opportunity to participate in the sport of fly fishing is a privilege and a responsibility. Fly anglers respect private property and always ask permission before entering or fishing private property. They seek to understand and follow the local customs and practices associated with the fishery. They share the waters equally with others whether they are fishing or engaging in other outdoor activities.

· Fly fishers minimize their impact on the environment and fishery by adopting practices that do not degrade the quality of the banks, waters, and the overall watersheds upon which fisheries depend. These practices include avoiding the introduction of species not native to an ecosystem, and cleaning and drying fishing gear to prevent the inadvertent transport of invasive exotics that may threaten the integrity of an aquatic ecosystem. In simplest terms, fly anglers always leave the fishery better than when they found it.

· Fly anglers endeavor to conserve fisheries by understanding the importance of limiting their catch. "Catch and release" is an important component of sustaining premium fisheries that are being over-harvested. Fly anglers release fish properly and with minimal harm. They promote the use of barbless hooks and angling practices that are more challenging but which help to sustain healthy fish populations.

· Fly anglers do not judge the methods of fellow anglers. Fly fishers share their knowledge of skills and techniques. They help others to understand that fly-fishing contributes to sound fisheries conservation practices.

· Fly anglers treat fellow anglers as they would expect to be treated. They do not impose themselves on or otherwise interfere with other anglers. They wait a polite time, and then, if necessary, request permission to fish through. They may invite other anglers to fish through their positions. Fly fishers when entering an occupied run or area always move in behind other anglers, not in front of them whether in a boat or wading.

· Fly anglers when sharing the water allow fellow

anglers ample room so as not to disturb anyone's fishing experience. They always fish in a manner that causes as little disturbance as practical to the water and fish. They take precautions to keep their shadow from falling across the water (walking a high bank).

· When fishing from watercraft fly anglers do not crowd other anglers or craft. They do not block entrances to bays or otherwise impede others. Fly anglers do not unnecessarily disturb the water by improperly lowering anchors or slapping the water with paddles or oars.

· Fly anglers always compliment other anglers and promote this Code of Angling Ethics to them whether they fish with a fly or not.

RHEA TOPPING

Some Dos, Don'ts, and Solutions

Crowding: The Biggest Problem

$\mathcal{F}$ly fishing is somewhat of a solitary sport. Comfort zones and space are key words.

1. If another angler is already fishing when you arrive:
   (a) Don't enter the water directly in front of him/her: Say, "excuse me, do you mind if I go in here?," and even then allow plenty of room. Only do this if there is no other

alternative. It would be better to find another spot in which to fish.

(b) Always notice and/or ask in which direction they are fishing.

(c) Give them plenty of space. How much space varies depending on the type of water and situation to situation. If you have to ask them if it's okay to fish there, you are too close.

(d) If two anglers are fishing moving water in the same direction, the faster wader should get out quietly, make a wide berth on the bank, and move far enough ahead of the slower angler to allow that person plenty of water to fish. If it's possible without making a disturbance, it would be courteous to let the slower angler know how far up you plan to start fishing again.

2. Wade quietly and slowly in company. Shock waves spook fish.

3. Fish where others aren't. Fish at less popular times of the day and week.

4. Watch those backcasts.

5. Leapfrog or rotate pools to share space. This is fun.

6. Learn to share space. If you can hear other anglers speaking in regular voices, you're too close. Go seek out a new spot and enjoy.

7. Never encroach on someone who is "into" fish, or disturb them by asking what fly pattern/technique they are using.

8. Attempt to "just let it slide" if there is no opportunity for peaceful negotiations. If one can point out the breach of etiquette in a civilized manner, perhaps that person won't be as inconsiderate or negligent on their next outing. And, it won't ruin the rest of your day having gotten into a confront.

Respect for Other Anglers

Stop, look, listen, and think. Ask yourself, Are my actions going to disturb someone else's precious time on the water?

Don't be quick to judge another angler's error—it may be simply a matter of ignorance.

1. Stay away from the banks. The vibration of your feet or your silhouette could spook fish.
2. Walk quietly past anglers in the water, giving them a wide berth.
3. Leave loud dogs, children, and loud music at home. Only make a lot of noise if you are about to be consumed by a grizzly bear, or jumped by a mountain lion.
4. Leave pets at home. If you have your dog along, make sure it doesn't interfere with anyone else's fishing.
5. If someone shares a secret spot with you, don't abuse that privilege by telling others or going back without that same someone's permission.
6. Don't whoop and carry on when you hook a fish—most people aren't interested in your success ratio. Respect their privacy and solitude.
7. If an angler is sitting on a bank, or is in a boat, not fishing, they may well be resting a fish. Don't barge in.
8. If someone offers you a fly from his or her box, reciprocate.
9. Don't look through anyone's fly boxes without permission, be it your guide or a friend.
10. Wade and paddle quietly—avoid spooking the fish.
11. Don't make fun of casting disasters unless they are your own.
12. Show equal respect for spin fishermen, boaters, and float tubers. It's their resource too.
13. Only give advice if you are asked for it.

14. It is acceptable to greet another angler and inquire about the fishing. It is also acceptable not to acknowledge them at all.

15. Cell phones, walkie talkies, beepers, etc., can be disturbing to others.

16. Mind your manners and language.

Some Options for Fishing in Crowds or with Friends
The Rotation System
The only time it is acceptable to cast into water being fished by other anglers is when using the *rotation system*. This practice is an equitable way for a number of anglers to share a pool, allowing everyone to get an equal chance at fishing the best holding water. This is a long accepted method in fishing for salmon and steelhead, as well as in the fall on the Madison River at the Barns Holes.

In this type of situation, the anglers want to cover as much water as quickly as possible. With a rotation system, the first angler, or anglers, to arrive at a section of holding water begin fishing it from the top. They wade in and cast across the currents, quartering downstream, most likely using wet flies or streamers. They make a cast, fish it out, perhaps make a few more casts, then take a step or two downstream. Eventually they will have covered the entire pool, wade out, and go back up to the top and begin again. Other anglers fall in behind, using the same system, and making room for several anglers. If the first angler moves a fish or misses a strike, they may continue to fish that spot for a few more casts. If they land a fish, they go back to the rear of the line.

Fishing a rotation still allows the first angler there to have the first and often best chance at each fish. However, unlike

The rotation system.

our accepted system in this country of "first come, first served," everyone gets a fair opportunity to fish the same good water.

If there are more anglers than the spot can hold, a line forms on the bank with each angler entering the water when his turn comes up. An angler who has already fished through the pool will go to the end of the line on the bank. The system usually works very smoothly, and many anglers look forward to this camaraderie. One may also fish dry flies, using the rotation in reverse, moving upstream.

On Sharing Smaller Water

When fishing with a friend or with two anglers, one can have fun either by fishing side by side, by taking turns casting to and spotting a fish, by sharing one rod, or by fishing from opposite banks, switching banks occasionally. Alternatively, if you want to fish "together" but have some space and solitude, one can "leap frog." This can be a successful and fun tactic for fishing smaller water with a friend. By splitting up and leapfrogging the pools, each angler gets a fair shot at a pool without being rushed or crowded. The secret to success is for both anglers to fish at the same pace and not waste too much time in unproductive water.

On Rights-of-Way

It would be so pleasant if, when encountering another angler, we all subscribed to the following unstated rules as to who has the right-of-way:

1. The angler fishing upstream.
2. The angler with a fish on.
3. Any stationary angler . . . the floating/boating angler should yield to the wading angler. Sometimes this doesn't work, so let it slide—remember, the folks in the "aluminum hatches" have water rights too.
4. The first angler to arrive and start fishing.

On the Environment

1. Pack it in, pack it out.
2. Don't make new trails; use the old ones when possible.
3. Try not to disturb the stream bottom, and replace rocks that you have turned over to examine for insects. *Never* use "the San Juan shuffle"(a stream-bottom dance that stirs up the insects and attracts the fish).
4. Avoid using lead. There are new materials on the market that work just fine.
5. Put your own, and picked up abandoned, fishing line (monofilament) and any other trash in your pocket to dispose of later.

Death by monofiliment.

6. Use environmentally friendly soaps and shampoos.

7. If you smoke, take your matches and cigarette butts with you.

8. Someone once said, "Take nothing but photographs; leave nothing but footprints."

On the Law

1. Buy and carry a license.

2. Don't trespass—not even to cross private property—without asking permission. Always close gates the way you found them.

3. Have respect for the high water marks.

4. Know your local and state regulations. Obey or pay.

    You are fishing with other anglers and someone starts poaching or keeping fish illegally—what do you do? Report them? Right. You know you should, but it's not easy: You're with friends; it's awkward; they might get angry or worse; and besides, it's only a fish or two.

Fine. Let's look at another situation: You're out hunting with friends, and one of them shoots a bald eagle or a trumpeter swan—what would you do then?

Try to talk to the offender and explain what they have done wrong and why it's wrong. If that fails, try to get their car tag and description. There are toll-free numbers to report the poaching of any animal or fish, or contact your local game warden or government agency. We need to keep one another honest and law abiding.

5. Encourage and support the enforcement officers.
6. Thank the landowner afterward. Be an ambassador for our sport.

On Boats

1. Never cut between another boat and a school of fish, or on a sand flat, between another boat and the fish it is working. Always idle off a flat far enough away from other boats so that you don't disturb the area.
2. Reel in your line if your partner has a fish on in a boat, or is fishing close by.
3. If you are operating a boat, look out for other people's lines, and other anglers. Some guides will get in the water and walk their boat behind their anglers to avoid spooking the fish downstream.
4. Keep your distance from a boat following a hooked fish.
5. Don't hog the bow: Take turns in the bow of a boat, either by fish count, solid hook up, or by setting a time limit. The angler in the stern is responsible for watching the angler in the bow, and timing his/her casts accordingly.
6. Try not to put down rising fish. Navigate well away from the angler into the middle of the river. And don't cast into their fish.

Wrong! Load gear into your boat before launching.

7. Have your boat prepped, gear already in the boat, and unload your boat quickly at a ramp to let others get in too.

8. Be careful of anchor/oar sounds and noise from hitting the side of the boat or tackle boxes banging inside the boat.

9. Check everything out ahead of time and make sure you know what you are getting into.

10. The first to arrive are the first to launch.

11. Since a stationary boat or a fisherman on shore disturbs less water than a moving boat, and a boat's wake can disturb the fishing, the moving boat should circle around the stationary anglers to pass.

12. New boaters should practice backing and launching during off times.

13. The boat moving upwind has the right-of-way, and a stationary boat should always be passed slowly and given a wide berth.

The Client's Responsibility to the Guide

1. If they are deserving, tip in cash: 15 to 20 percent is a rule of thumb. Please don't tip in free meals.
2. On a charter boat, tip the mate directly, and don't give it all to the skipper.
3. Treat your guide like a friend, not an employee. Respect his knowledge of his water.
4. Be on time.
5. Make sure your needs and wants are clear ahead of time, i.e., your expectations, your level of expertise, the type of fishing you prefer (wading or floating, wet or dry flies, many fish or trophy fish, etc.). Specify your dietary and drink preferences for lunch, and whether you want some instruction and/or to have some "alone time."
6. Easier to say than to do, but if you are displeased with your guide, tell either him or the shop why, and reflect it in your tip.

The Guide's Responsibility to the Client

1. Find out the level of expertise.
2. Review safety issues.
3. Ask their fishing preferences (dry/wet, wade/float, some instruction, etc.).
4. Ask if they mind a lot of walking, and when they need to be back.
5. Ask about meal/drink requests, or let them know if you expect them to supply their own, and also yours. In cold conditions hot tea, coffee, or soup is well received.
6. Check their fly patterns and specify whether they need to buy more, or if you will supply them. Additionally, let them know if they will be charged for them.

7. Specify necessary equipment in advance (gear, sunglasses, etc.).
8. Put yourself in the client's wading boots.
9. *Never* take a client's rod or your own and fish—unless they insist.
10. Either the guide or the shop should let the client know in advance what is not included in the guide fee (tips, leaders, flies, etc.).
11. Respect silence—avoid constant chatter between two guides.
12. Know your business, as well as some history of the area, the fauna, and the flora.

———— ∞ ————

"Treat our lands and waters, the treasures therein, each other and yourself with respect."—Mel Krieger

AFTERWORD

In my opinion, etiquette is far more important today than teaching students to cast effectively, to read water, to tie good knots, to catch fish. For in this ever-more-crowded world of fly fishing, if we forget our "water manners," it's all lost.

Perhaps no one has said it any more succinctly than Roderick Haig-Brown in his essay "Outdoor Ethics":

> "I submit first of all that there is no such thing as sport without ethics.
>
> Ethics are a morality beyond the demands of the law. And, from traditional ethics a more complicated system of ethics grows and builds. There is one guiding spirit—attitude of mind, and it has three major directions. One, consideration for your fellow sportsmen. Two, consideration for fish and wildlife stock. Three, consideration for the land and water upon which they and the sport depend. These are things that have to be taught from the very beginning. If they are taught and properly understood, more specific codes of ethics will inevitably grow from them.
>
> You cannot legislate successfully against the jealous fisherman who spoils the sport of others as well as his own. You have to train him. You can teach the spirit of generosity; you can establish codes—written or unwritten—that will, in time, find general acceptance and attain a moral force more powerful than the law.
>
> You cannot do this in a week or a year, but it can be

done over a period of years, if we, as leaders, tighten our own standards, define them more carefully, and pass the results on to others. This is precisely what will be needed as more and more people go out into the woods and onto the waters to find satisfaction in their own particular way. Ethics, though they accept the law and abide by it, are, as I said at the beginning, a morality beyond the demands of the law."

My sincere hope for the future of angling is that novice and expert, park services and fly shops, boat rental agencies and guides, fly fishers and spin fishers, and every one of us who loves the sport will pass this concept on.

Teach all this to our children.
They are the caretakers of the future.

Take nothing but photographs; leave nothing but footprints.

PHOTO AND ILLUSTRATION CREDITS

Baughman, Michael, "The Gentleman at Fairview," from *A River Seen Right—A Fly Fisherman's North Umpqua*. Lyons and Burford, 1995. Reprinted with the permission of The Lyons Press.

Bergman, Ray, "Angling Ethics and Conclusion," from *Just Fishing*. Penn Publishing Co., 1932. Reprinted with the permission of *Outdoor Life* magazine, courtesy of Jerry Gibb.

Berners, Dame Juliana, "Treatyse of Fysshynge with an Angle," from *The Origins of Angling*. Copyright 1997 by John McDonald. Reprinted with the permission of The Lyons Press.

Bradshaw, Stan, "River Etiquette in Dry Times," from *River Safety: A Floater's Guide*. Greycliff Publishing, 2000. Reprinted with the permission of the author.

Brooks, Joe, "Stream Manners and Safety," from *The Complete Book of Fly Fishing*. Copyright 1998 Outdoor Life Books. Reprinted with the permission of the Joe Brooks estate, courtesy of Cam Sigler.

Burton, Mallory, "Messing With the River Gods," from *Reading the Water: Stories and Essays of Flyfishing and Life*. Copyright 1995 by Mallory Burton. Reprinted with the permission of Keokee Co. Publishing, Inc. Available from the publisher at 1-800-880-3573 or on the web at www.KeokeeBooks.com.

Evanoff, Vlad, "Problems," from *Surf Fishing*. A. S. Barnes & Co., Inc., 1948.

Grant, Gary, "Goals, Codes, and Rules of the Rod." Copyright 2002 by the Federation of Fly Fishers, Inc. Reprinted by permission.

Haig-Brown, Roderick, "Articles of Faith for Good Anglers." Copyright 1960 Roderick Haig-Brown. Reprinted by permission of Harold Ober Associates, Incorporated, and courtesy of Valerie Haig-Brown.

Haig-Brown, Roderick, extract from "Outdoor Ethics." Reprinted by permission of Harold Ober Associates, Incorporated, and courtesy of Valerie Haig-Brown.

Horton Manufacturing Company, "Etiquette Among Fishermen," from *Tricks and Knacks of Fishing*. Copyright 1911 by Horton Mfg. Co.

Jindra, Tom, "Rethinking Conservation and the Ocean," from *Fly Fish America* magazine, 1998. Reprinted with the permission of the author.

Kreider, Claude M., "The Steelhead Angler's Attitude and Ethics," from *Steelhead*. G. P. Putnam & Sons, 1948.

Kustich, Jerry, "P.S. Out Fishing," from *Fly Fisherman* magazine. Reprinted with the permission of the author.

Kyte, Al, "In Search of Etiquette," from *California Fly Fisher*, September 1994. Reprinted with the permission of *California Fly Fisher*, courtesy of Richard Anderson.

LaFontaine, Gary, "Fishing Among the Barbarians." From *The Book Mailer,* 1997. Reprinted with the permission of *The Book Mailer*, courtesy of Stan Bradshaw.

Law, Glenn, "Fishing Manners in the United Kingdom," from *A Concise History of Fly Fishing*, The Lyons Press, 2003. Reprinted with the permission of the author.

Lyons, Nick, "Crowds," from *The Flyfisher's World*, 1995. Reprinted with the permission of The Atlantic Monthly Press, courtesy of Mary Flower.

McGuane, Tom, excerpts from *The Longest Silence*. Alfred A. Knopf, 2000. Reprinted with the permission of the author.

National Marine Fisheries Service, "Code of Angling Ethics." Reprinted with the permission of the NMFS, courtesy of John Ross.

Parsons, P. Allen, "The Fisherman's Ethics," from *The Complete Book of Freshwater Fishing*. Reprinted with the permission of *Outdoor Life* magazine for Outdoor Life Books, a division of Harper & Row, courtesy of Jerry Gibb.

Phair, Charles, "Protecting and Stocking Salmon Rivers," from *Atlantic Salmon Fishing*, Derrydale Press, 1937.

Quick, James, "Sportsmen's Ethics," from *Trout Fishing and Trout Flies*. Copyright 1957 Countryman Press, by arrangement with A. S. Barnes & Co., Inc.

Scharff, Robert, "Etiquette for Fishermen," from *Esquire's Book of Fishing*. Harper & Row, 1962.

Schramm, Dorothy, excerpt from *The Flygirls Newsletter,* September 1998. Reprinted with the permission of the author.

Schwiebert, Ernest, "Ethics, Manners, and Philosophy Astream," from *Trout*. E. P. Dutton, 1978. Reprinted with permission of the author.

Slaymaker, Samuel R. II, "Ten Commandments of Stream Etiquette," from *Simplified Fly Fishing*. Harper & Row, 1962.

Swisher, Doug and Carl Richards, "Stream Courtesy," from *Fly Fishing Strategy*. Crown Publishers, 1975. Reprinted with the permission of the authors.

Talleur, Dick, excerpts from *Fly Fishing for Trout*. Winchester Press, 1974. Reprinted with the permission of the author.

———∞∞∞———